Praise for *The Art of Product Design*

"The communications revolution created by the Internet is breaking down barriers between countries as well as companies, enabling talented individuals everywhere to find opportunities around the globe. The GrabCAD community is a story of how smart, creative people from around the world can find each other; solve problems, old and new; and do amazing things."

—**Toomas Hendrik Ilves,** President of Estonia

"Hardi does a nice job of amplifying the underlying trends that are revolutionizing the mechanical product development process. At Kiva Systems, we experienced these forces at work while designing and delivering four versions of our robot in four years—leveraging a broad community of interconnected designers and suppliers, working virtually and across continents, then physically, sometimes with next-day overnight deliveries. The power of this radically new world always hit home when we booted up the first prototype and it 'just worked' as designed. Hardi's book is a must-read for executives in and around physical product development—disrupt or be disrupted."

—**Mick Mountz, CEO and founder,** Kiva Systems

"Hardi tells two fascinating stories with this book, one about how he founded and grew GrabCAD and the other about how he sees the world of product design changing. Both stories are relevant to anyone seeking to take advantage of new online communities and connections to grow their business."

—**Dean Kamen,** founder of DEKA
Research and Development Corporation

"The online community Hardi and his team have created is a great example of how today's unprecedented access to technology, content, and people is changing the way we make things."

—**Carl Bass,** CEO of Autodesk

"Listen to the stories you find in *The Art of Design* about the next industrial revolution and you'll be ready for the future—Hardi has his hand on the pulse of what happens next in the 3D design world."

—**Bre Prettis,** CEO of Makerbot Inc.

The Art of Product Design

Changing How Things Get Made

Hardi Meybaum

WILEY

Library of Congress Cataloging-in-Publication Data:

Meybaum, Hardi.
    The art of product design : changing how things get made / Hardi Meybaum.
        pages   cm
    Includes index.
    ISBN 978-1-118-76334-6 (cloth); ISBN 978-1-118-88103-3 (ebk);
    ISBN 978-1-118-88104-0 (ebk)
        1. Product design—Technological innovations.   I. Meybaum, Hardi.   II. Title.
    TS171.4.M49   2014
    658.5'752—dc23

                                                            2013046064

Printed in the United States of America

10 9 8 7 6 5 4 3 2 1

CONTENTS

INTRODUCTION
THE DIGITAL REVOLUTION
GETS PHYSICAL

Over the past 30 years, anything and everything that needs no physical form has been reduced to bits. Music, photographs, newspapers, plane tickets, and money have all gone digital. Soon, with driverless cars on the horizon, even taxi drivers may be transformed from flesh into software.

By comparison, change in things that must remain physical has been almost glacial: How we design and make stuff today—hardware, manufactured goods—is not radically different from what it was in 1980. And sadly, in the so-called post–industrial age, making things has been downright uncool. Intangibles such as software and finance have been where it's at.

But that's about to change—and very quickly.

Powerful forces are converging to drive a second great wave of the digital revolution. Where the first wave was about shedding physical form, the second wave exponentially amplifies our ability to create physical form, in any shape or size to any end we can imagine. In the process, it radically reorders all our notions about making things: who designs and who builds; how fast, where, and at what scale; and how is it marketed?

It's not simply a matter of making new things we never dreamed of. This revolution comes with the opportunity to refashion thousands of everyday objects, making them smarter, greener, and connected with the surrounding environment. And now is precisely the time to do that as technological viability converges with surging demand for solutions for critical challenges ranging from spiraling health care costs to global warming.

It's a revolution fueled by the monumental waste—waste of time, energy, and health, both human and ecological—that is built into our current technology. It's about red traffic lights at midnight: the oceans of motor fuel we emit and the millions of minutes we waste while stopped at them, even when there's no traffic. It's about the millions of pounds of cure we administer where nano-ounces of preventive health care would do. It's about the millions who still die needlessly in car crashes despite our having to endure red lights at midnight.

There is a humongous load of needlessly stupid stuff in this world that needs to be fixed, not "when we get around to it," but right *now*.

If waste fuels this revolution, an explosion of creativity drives it forward. At its very core are epoch-making new tools that dramatically eliminate the barriers between human inspiration and physical reality. If you can imagine something that you know will work—*anything*—you can now build it, virtually if not physically.

The revolution takes shape as creators awake to the vast potential these tools unlock. It moves forward as creators pioneer new ways to organize human genius and effort around the new tools. It accelerates with passion and excitement, from the earnest desire to solve problems great and small to the eternal quest for human delight, be it high art or street-cool. And, of course, there's the scent of profit, too. There is definitely money in all this.

You may have already noticed aspects of what's happening without realizing how the pieces fit together: New products appear in months instead of years, three-dimensional (3D) printers are in the news, hardware start-ups are sprouting up in unlikely places with crowdfunded capital, and talk of a "maker's movement" ensues.

Behind all these innovations are new tools that have matured and proliferated over the past 30 years with surprisingly little notice beyond the disciplines of design and engineering. They are the tools that now allow small start-ups to sprout up by achieving in mere months feats of technology that would have taken an army of engineers years to complete in the 1960s. They are the source of stunningly realistic visualizations that now draw investors from the crowd. They are the brains that precisely instruct those 3D printers. And they are what makes the maker's movement more than just a hipster notion.

Collectively, these tools are functions of three-dimensional computer-aided design, or 3D CAD as we call it. In this book you will learn why I believe historians will one day rank 3D CAD alongside Gutenberg's printing press among truly epoch-making technologies.

Skip to the absolutely essential thing to grasp about 3D CAD today: It concentrates unprecedented and phenomenal creative power on the designer's screen, at the point where ideas takes shape, at the very top of the process that results in manufactured objects. And it projects that creative power through every stage of the process: from design through capital fund-raising, prototyping, market research, and manufacturing, all the way down to marketing.

From the earliest inception of an idea, CAD eliminates abstraction by generating a three-dimensional virtual reality that is as quickly malleable as the clay on a potter's wheel—and globally communicable with total fidelity at broadband speed. Via highly realistic 3D renderings, anyone anywhere can see instantly and exactly what the object is meant to do and provide feedback. What's more, via highly comprehensive numerical instructions, CAD can precisely instruct those who manufacture the object.

Here's where we arrive at a key point of convergence. Those highly comprehensive numerical instructions that CAD generates are written in the language understood by robots and other increasingly sophisticated automated factory tools. From the designer's screen to the factory floor—be it in China or Chicago—nothing is lost in translation.

In a nutshell, this is what makes 3D CAD pivotal in the second and physical wave of the digital revolution. But why is its impact only now becoming apparent? That's the story this book is going to tell.

The first short answer is that, until now, 3D CAD has developed essentially as four archipelagos of unconnected islands. Four giant vendors have sold expensive and mutually incompatible systems, mainly to corporate customers, that have kept them strictly isolated behind firewalls. This setup allowed automakers and aerospace companies to make huge strides with gargantuan enterprise systems, but it meant that CAD remained largely a corporate phenomenon. For years its revolutionary potential did not extend far beyond the immediate supply chains of large companies.

That started to change over the past decade as increasingly sophisticated capability began to come within reach of small enterprises and individuals by way of (still expensive) installed software. Even so, CAD users remained relatively isolated from one another, relying on e-mail or file transfer services to pass around huge files—hardly what you could call an ecosystem.

This is where our story begins, as several trends began to converge circa 2010.

First, cloud computing began to make it possible for those huge CAD files to reside on a server where all stakeholders could securely access them. Even better, creators started to realize that the cloud would enable them to focus massive compute power on the objects in these files—crash testing, for example. All this made people start to ask why it made sense to use expensive installed programs when they could be using always-up-to-date, pay-as-you-go software in the cloud. People suddenly saw through the emperor's new clothes.

Second, like a dissipating fog, the uncool stigma around hardware began to lift. Seemingly out of nowhere, trendsetters in places such as Silicon Valley began to talk about "makers."

Third, as I discovered, there was growing unmet demand among CAD users for community, for some way to bridge the gaps between tens of thousands of individual engineers and designers who were exploring their still newfound capabilities.

In 2010 I cofounded GrabCAD.com as an online community that allows 3D CAD users to share their designs and learn from one another. In just three years our community has grown from a small village to a metropolis with more than one million members—more than one-third of the world's 3D

CAD users. It's become an intense global community, buzzing with experimentation and imagination.

Imagine is, in fact, the key word, because now the playing field tilts toward creators and designers. Although technological innovation opens the gate to this revolution, its motive power isn't in the tools. It's in the individual genius they unlock. It's in the new forms of networked collaboration they enable. It's in devolving to individuals and small teams the ability to design, perfect, and fabricate any object they choose to create.

The tools are now in hand, and imaginations are fired up. What is only now beginning to develop are new models of social organization better suited to a product development and manufacturing process that will be vastly different from the models developed through the age of mass production.

What will these new social models look like? Will giant companies be toppled by small, agile, crowdfunded start-ups? Will design and manufacturing become completely divorced? Or will new verticals emerge, with CAD designers directly instructing completely automated production? Will unskilled factory labor disappear? If labor cost becomes less decisive, will manufacturing activity leave China as fast as it arrived? And where will it go if it does?

Everything we currently take for granted about product design, development, and manufacturing is now up in the air. Where it finally comes to rest will have huge implications for investors, businesspeople, workers, and national economies.

As the revolution unfolds, only a couple of things are certain. One is that "the Force" will be with teams—big or small—with the binary combination of powerful imagination and the collective skills needed to elaborate it accurately and quickly.

The other certainty is that imagination is available from only one source: the inspired brains of individual human beings. That's why this revolution will be driven from the grassroots up, by engineers and designers with the full binary package.

This book tells the story of this revolution, with a focus on the "inspired brains" I mentioned. And while many of those brains reside in engineers and designers, I think the lessons are important to anyone involved in making, selling, or even buying things, which is to say, all of us. To help make the connection between the engineering world and the more general business world, I've included at the end of each chapter a list of "Executive Takeaways" that spells out ways I think executives and other business people can take action.

And who am I to tell you all this? As the host of a remarkable online community, I have a ringside seat on the revolution. And in the following chapters I will share what I have seen so far.

1 Gearheads Get No Respect

Look around you. Unless you're in an antique shop, almost any manufactured object you see was created by a mechanical engineer using computer-aided design (CAD) software. Like a cowboy and his horse, object creators and their three-dimensional (3D) CAD tools are almost inseparable today, so much so that after a long week working on CAD at the office, many will head straight to the basement after dinner on Friday to dive right back into CAD, working all weekend long on their hobby projects.

They are driven by a specific kind of intelligence and a particular passion. Much more than just a job, mechanical engineering is a calling that summons many of us in the sandbox. When asked what got them started, one gearhead after another will tell you something like: "I took apart every toy I got until they gave me LEGO. Then I started putting things together and never stopped."

It's good they have that passion driving them, because if it was all about glory, no one would pursue a career in mechanical engineering.

You see these engineers' accomplishments everywhere, in innovations that drive economic growth and make the world a safer, greener, and more efficient place. But compared with the stars of other professions, such as architecture or design or medicine, mechanical engineers mostly toil away in quiet obscurity. It has always been rare to see an engineer profiled in the media (except perhaps in *Popular Mechanics*). In recent post–industrial age decades, gearheads have moved even further from the limelight than ever. After all, manufacturing is so twentieth century.

This isn't to say that mechanical engineers sit around moaning about how they get no respect—that's for lawyers. Who needs recognition when you were in one of the world's most stable professions anyway? No one with a mechanical engineering degree was ever short of a job.

That began to change in the 1990s, as shifts in industrial activity led to the emergence of rust belts—first in the United States, Europe, and the former Soviet Union and later in Japan. With less opportunity available close to home, mechanical engineers began to feel a need to look over the horizon for work. Fortunately, the development of CAD around the same time began to make it possible for engineering work to be done remotely.

But where do you go to find engineering work on the other side of the globe? And how do you make contact with like-minded engineers around the corner and across the world?

Love at First Sight

In my own case, the call summoning me to mechanical engineering did not come until I was in high school. I was in tenth grade when, like a young cowboy, I saw my first horse. It was 1998 when I first set my eyes on a 3D CAD program, which was then still a recent innovation. It was love at first sight.

In a single moment, CAD brought my fascination with information technology (fueled by an aptitude for math and physics) together with my delight in tinkering with physical objects, propelling me toward a career in mechanical engineering.

For the next 10 years I was happy to do nothing else. But fascination begins to wear thin once you find yourself endlessly tweaking the same set of variables. Instead of building the Ferraris and spaceships of my dreams, five years into my career as a professional engineer I woke up one day to the dull reality of a routine job. Trapped in a tiny market and bored, I hit the wall. So I decided to write an app to get me over the wall . . . and this is what happened.

Getting over the Wall

I'm from Estonia, the tiny Baltic country that Stalin swallowed like a single shot of vodka—and tried to digest with a decades-long campaign of Russification. Escape from the Soviet empire seemed like an unlikely dream, so as kids growing up in Tallinn, we just watched the West with envy via secret antennas tuned into Finnish television stations 70 kilometers across the Baltic in Helsinki. I learned English by watching James Bond movies with English subtitles. We used to practice lines like "shaken not stirred."

Miracle of miracles, though, as the Soviet Union disintegrated after the Berlin Wall fell in 1989, we managed to regain our independence in 1991. I was nine years old when our little nation of 1.4 million people started over from zero as a capitalist society. It was almost like the beginning of a game of Monopoly, when the bank deals out the same amount of money to each player. Each man, woman, and child in Estonia was allowed to convert 1,500 rubles for 150 kroon, our newly minted currency. This amount was equal to only a day's blue-collar wage in Finland, but it was like magic to hold our own money.

Having wages much lower than Finland was actually convenient because Helsinki—one hour from Tallinn by ferry—was in the midst of an economic boom as it joined the European Union and Nokia emerged as the global leader in GSM mobile telephony. Even better, because Estonian is perhaps as close to Finnish as Spanish is to Portuguese, we can easily understand what the Finns are on about. (Don't worry if you can't understand the Finns, you're not missing much.)

So overnight Estonia became Finland's Mexico, a low-cost outsourcing platform right next door. That created opportunity for people in Estonia with a wide range of industrial skills, but engineers were in short supply. And given how quickly technology was changing, recent engineering graduates had a huge advantage, especially those with information technology (IT) knowledge.

To tell you this will make me sound like grandfather recounting how tough life was during the war, but to catch up with the West in IT, we really had to work at it. When I was a child, all we had was a very expensive dial-up connection to the Internet, so my father used to strictly limit my time online to just half an hour each day. Not all bad, it forced me to learn as much as I could in the short time I had.

In any case, I was working part-time as an apprentice before I finished engineering school. As soon as I received my diploma, I started to work full-time with Saku Metall, Estonia's largest door maker and a key subcontractor for Kone, the Finnish elevator maker. By age 24, I was promoted to head of the IT department and made responsible for automating a wide range of engineering functions. It was a fun challenge and an exciting time.

Across town, meanwhile, my friends were developing Skype—the Internet-based telephony system that is Estonia's greatest contribution to human civilization, at least so far.

Engineers in our small city with just 400,000 people were doing outsourced work for clients all around the world.

If we got any respect, though, it was kind of backhanded. The *Dilbert* comic by Scott Adams continues to make fun of outsource engineers in "Elbonia," apparently a corruption of our country's name. In response, let me paraphrase Lynyrd Skynyrd: "I hope Scott Adams will remember, an Elbonian man don't need him around anyhow."

All the same, by 2008 I was bored with making doors and eager to play in a bigger league. So with a friend I set about creating a simple website aimed at offering 3D CAD service to clients around the world. The idea was that customers could upload rough design drawings to our site, which would then automatically generate a price quote.

Not knowing anything at all about business, we promised whatever we could think of that might attract customers. Maybe "satisfaction or your money back" was not a bad idea. But "24-hour turnaround" is a foolish promise to make if clients don't actually need it that fast. We lost a lot of sleep as a result. Our pricing was even dumber because we had absolutely no idea what things cost in the West—such as how much people are willing to pay for a cappuccino at Starbucks. So we offered to do CAD simple drawings for just $25 each.

To emphasize our speedy service, we called it GrabCAD.

The day the site went live in November 2009, we bought a $20 Google ad and sat watching our computer screens like a pair of ice fishermen looking down their hole in the lake. It took an entire week for the first order to come in: rough drawings of an ATV wheelbarrow from a man in Texas. We spent 12 hours frantically working on the CAD file, and for our efforts we got $55.

Three months later, you can imagine my family's reaction when I quit my day job, one week before the birth of my first daughter. Luckily my wife, Laura, supported me then, and every step of the way since. Meanwhile, my parents, my friends, and my colleagues all lined up to tell me one after the other that I was irresponsible and immature, if not clinically insane.

Perhaps I am. But whatever else I might be, I'm stubborn.

The GrabCAD vision began to evolve. We were fixated by the idea that we were building a service business, yet we realized that we were not going to get very far by staying up all night every night doing the work ourselves. Nor did we have the resources to hire a roomful of full-time CAD designers . We scratched our heads trying to think up new ways to create a scalable marketplace by attracting freelancers and moonlighters whose services we could sell to clients.

It was almost as an afterthought that in August 2010 we added what has turned out to be the magic feature that has grown our community into a million engineers and designers: an online place where CAD practitioners could share their designs.

Within a month we had almost 1,000 engineers using our site, and a vision began to form in my head: an online community that would give engineers easy access to sophisticated tools and allow them to collaborate seamlessly—and how all of this would revolutionize the making of physical objects.

Beware of getting a big idea.

Because 95 percent of our users were in the United States, I began to think, "Why am I here in Estonia if all the users are American?" Or, as Toyota engineers say, "*genchi genbutsu*"—don't rely on second-hand data; go straight to the source. In any event,

I really wanted to go America because it's the Mecca of CAD. I persuaded my wife to let me take a chunk of our meager savings and managed to get a three-month tourist visa for the United States. In October 2010, I flew to America with my family.

What I Discovered in America

When I arrived I was 28 years old, I had just $3,000 in my pocket (which was supposed to last us three months), and I didn't know a soul. At least I could speak almost enough English to explain the ideas that were bouncing around in my head.

Where should I go in such a big country? Of course, for anyone in IT it is *de rigueur* to make a pilgrimage to the holy Silicon Valley, but where else? I decided on Boston because it is the epicenter of the CAD industry and home to the legendary Massachusetts Institute of Technology (MIT). That's why I resolved to spend six weeks on each coast.

If you believe the conventional wisdom, Silicon Valley is supposed to be a freewheeling culture with no hierarchy, a place where your ideas matter and your pedigree doesn't. Boston, by contrast, is seen (at least from California) as "all uptight and Eastern," filled with preppies like the Winklevoss brothers of Facebook fame and open only to people with Ivy League degrees. I had none of this baggage when I arrived in Boston; no preconceived ideas. So after installing the family in a cheap motel in Framingham, 20 miles out in the suburbs, I just began contacting people out of the blue.

In Europe, if you try reaching out to people without an introduction or any sort of impressive credentials usually they don't even bother to reply. So in Boston I was delighted to find that even very busy and important people would respond to a cold call from a random Estonian by saying, "Please come and see me tomorrow."

When we met, they listened with kind interest and usually offered to introduce me to others. In this way, doors opened to me everywhere I went. I met many of the top players in the CAD industry and was able to visit MIT's amazing Media Lab.

I'm happy to report that several of the Bostonians I met in those first six weeks are still with me today, as friends and business associates. So don't ever try to tell me that Boston is a cold and snobbish place.

Silicon Valley was a completely different experience. It would not be fair to tar everyone I met with the same brush, but I encountered a lot of what felt like superficial bonhomie. To get ahead in California you have to come across as friendly and open, even if you're not. And because a lot of people are into their own "trips," they are not really interested in yours—at least until you are a "somebody." So you meet people who look over your shoulder as you talk, and what you say goes in one ear and out the other.

Maybe it was just because I was talking about hardware, physical objects, and manufactured goods. In 2010, hardware was deeply uncool in Silicon Valley and no one really wanted to know about it. The attitude was different in Boston perhaps because, with MIT and the CAD industry, physical stuff never stopped mattering there.

All the same, attitudes in Silicon Valley have changed dramatically in just three years as the maker's movement has become fashionable. Now every South of Market hipster has a riff about how 3D printers are going to change the world.

Perhaps we should give them all pocket protectors, the ultimate gearhead fashion accessory.

The end of 2010 was, however, about the worst time in history to talk about manufacturing in America. Two years after Lehman collapsed, the U.S. economy was still on hold and the mood was glum. General Motors and Chrysler had declared bankruptcy a year earlier, and engineering work was sliding offshore to China along with manufacturing.

As a consequence, mechanical engineers in places such as Michigan were desperately unemployed and unable to move because, with mortgages underwater, their houses were unsellable. All across the country, anyone who had an engineering job was clinging to it, no matter how boring—but maybe longing for something more.

Thinking about the plight of these people—many of them brilliant and highly experienced—brought home the truth that it was not just me in far-off Estonia who felt constrained by the circumstances of my location. Something was missing in the lives of mechanical engineers everywhere.

Not that any of this mattered to the venture capitalists I talked to about funding GrabCAD, at least not until I said the magic words: *social media*. Then they leaned forward in their chairs to listen. Hardware was nowhere, but social media was the flavor of the day. Social media for engineers? Why not?

Executive Takeaways

- Forget what people say about low-hanging fruit; aim high. Go beyond your comfort zone. Go in the opposite direction from the crowd if you want to find truly new opportunities.

- Don't automatically believe the conventional wisdom when you get there. People told me Boston was cold and snobbish.

- If you are trying to foster entrepreneurship in your organization, think about this: Would you take a meeting with a random Estonian who cold-called you?

2 Since the Potter's Wheel, the Most Important Tool in History

Is it possible to overstate the historic importance of 3D CAD?

That would be a stretch, because you have to go back to pre-history to find the advent of any tool that has given humans such a quantum leap in our ability to produce physical objects . . . maybe iron implements or the potter's wheel. Certainly, this marvel should rank somewhere alongside Gutenberg's printing press in the annals of technology.

If you have overlooked its significance until now, there is no shame in that. Since this still-new technology became widespread in the 1990s, it has largely been out of sight, hidden behind the locked doors of giant aerospace and automotive concerns and on the computers of individual engineers who don't usually make headlines.

Why do I venture to make such bold claims? What magical powers does 3D CAD give us?

To understand, you must first grasp what we gained in the leap from two to three dimensions.

For centuries, engineers designed in two dimensions, drafting and redrafting blueprints by hand. We could make sense of what we were creating, but it was working in abstract—and it was extremely labor-intensive.

Once two-dimensional (2D) CAD proliferated in the 1980s, the process of drafting and modifying blueprints became much more efficient—but it was still working in a 2D abstraction.

Today, working in three dimensions means no more abstraction. What we design on our screens is virtually the actual object. We can easily create the precise geometry of any shape we can imagine, from scratch or by scanning the contours of an existing object. We can examine it from any angle on the screen and modify the shape at will, as if we were potters working in clay.

Beyond the object's shape, we can attribute an extensive range of qualities to any part or surface. For example, we can make one part a certain metal alloy with specific properties: mass, hardness, flexibility, heat expansion and contraction, corrosion resistance, surface appearance, and more. We can mate that part with others that have completely different properties, perhaps composites or plastics. Then, with a click, we can see how they interact.

We can illustrate the assembly to show how the parts fit together. We can animate the working of the finished design to see all the moving parts in action and test its performance.

Every year we gain new capabilities to test our virtual prototypes against any criterion or simulated condition you can imagine: wind tunnels, temperature extremes (such as reentering the atmosphere), corrosion, crash damage, material cost, manufacturability—you name it. If we don't have it already, it is coming.

Equally critical is the ability to visually render designs from concept through completion. Back in the blueprint era, engineers had to bring in artists to sketch what were often crude impressions of the concept taking shape on the drafting table. Now, with a simple click we can render highly precise imagery in order to bring stakeholders—management, prospective customers, and investors—into the design loop. And this has led to an unforeseen blossoming of creativity: Matter-of-fact mechanical engineers have metamorphosed into passionate visual artists.

Once the design is ready to be transformed from virtual to physical, 3D CAD's comprehensive and precise trove of digital data can be used to directly instruct numerically controlled machines—such as 3D printers—capable of producing prototypes or finished products.

Until that final stage, the entire design process is now virtual and paperless. At its most elaborate, 3D CAD has become the indispensable tool for designing today's ultra-high-tech aircraft and automobiles. But most of the same capabilities are now also within reach of any individual creator who has a reasonably good computer, CAD software, the skill to use it . . . and a powerful imagination.

The creative power that 3D CAD puts in a single pair of hands, or a small team, is—to me at least—awe inspiring. And I'm confident that history will indeed one day rank it alongside Gutenberg's press.

Where did these amazing tools spring from? Who makes them?

If you are not already a CAD aficionado, you will need a quick crash course to make sense of the rest of this book. So here it is. . . .

CAD History from the Cavemen in a Nutshell

The first crude CAD tools were developed in tandem with the earliest mainframes from the 1940s. They now seem almost paleolithic.

It was not until the 1960s that halfway sophisticated 2D tools began to proliferate in the aerospace and automotive industries, often developed in-house. Although they delivered significant efficiencies, the early programs aimed only at automating blueprint production, making it easier to modify designs without completely redrawing the entire blueprint. Most engineers continued to use slide rules and early scientific calculators as they created blueprints at their drafting boards.

Over the three decades since 1969—the epic year in the history of technology when man landed on the moon—CAD technology progressed from horse and buggy to Saturn rocket. In fact, the development of CAD can only be understood in the context of the United States–Soviet space race, given the pivotal role of the aerospace industry.

(Incidentally, to me it seems that American taxpayers have no idea how much of a dividend they continue to reap from their 1960s investment in space exploration.)

Ironically, though, the history of CAD development reads more like the Old Testament—so-and-so begat so-and-so; this guy slew (or acquired) that guy—as software vendors and hardware makers rose and fell like Biblical empires. Names such as Digital Equipment Corporation (DEC), Structural Dynamics Research Corporation (SDRC), Control Data, and Computervision rose to dominate the landscape, then disappeared overnight, leaving barely a trace.

And although I would gladly honor the father of CAD like a saint, the search for a Moses is futile. Instead of one prophet who pointed the way, CAD seems to have had more fathers than a litter of kittens. But luminaries like Patrick Hanratty, Ivan Sutherland, and Charles Lang deserve to be recognized among the pioneers, and praise be to them.

It is equally ironic that the struggle to lead in 3D CAD was itself fought in three dimensions. The first dimension was a race to advance the capability of the software itself. The second was the race in compute power that took CAD from mainframe to laptop. The third was the competition to win customer business. Only those who could win consistently in all three dimensions survived. You had to have the leading design capability over a two- to three-year window, perfectly synchronized with the compute power customers had available at that time—and you had to be able to sell it. Get any of these wrong and you were out of the running.

DEC, for example, had a massive share of the hardware market for workstations that evaporated overnight when CAD migrated to the personal computer (PC).

Actually, there was a fourth dimension: leadership in large corporate systems where billion-dollar contracts were commonplace.

Chronologically, though, the game was fought in a succession of distinct periods.

The 1970s was the heyday of 2D CAD on mainframe computers, used by large engineering concerns to generate blueprints. As the technology proliferated, it spurred the development of a CAD industry, both software and hardware, that grew over the decade from revenues of $25 million to nearly $1 billion.

From the early 1980s, "minicomputers" enabled a wider range of engineering professionals to use increasingly sophisticated 2D CAD products. This is when DEC ruled in hardware.

But by the mid-1980s, UNIX workstations had cut the ground from under DEC's feet. The first PCs were also proliferating, although early models such as the IBM AT and XT had nowhere near enough power to run CAD programs. At the same time, the first really useful 3D CAD programs began to appear, notably CATIA from France's Dassault Systèmes (established in 1981). When Boeing selected CATIA as its core engineering tool in 1984, it was a landmark in the industry.

The competitive field was crowded in the latter half of the 1980s as a plethora of start-ups arrived on the scene. Looking back, only two really mattered: Autodesk, founded in 1982 by John Walker in Northern California, and Boston-based Parametric Technologies, founded in 1985 and known today as PTC.

Apart from Dassault, Autodesk, and PTC, the only other 1980s player worth remembering is the CAD offshoot of McDonnell Douglas. Known variously as Unigraphics or UGS, it has been passed from mega-corporate hand to hand over the years, first to Electronic Data Systems (EDS), when that company was owned by General Motors. Today, it survives as the CAD business of Germany's Siemens.

The breakthrough event that signaled the real onset of the 3D CAD era was Parametric's 1987 launch of Pro/Engineer. Running on the UNIX workstation, Pro/Engineer set the standard for modeling performance at a price far below competitive offerings. This gave the company a jump-start to the front rank of the industry, where it remains to this day.

Workstation-based 3D CAD offered amazing performance in that era, but as it still involved a hefty up-front investment, not every boy got one for Christmas. Which is to say, it remained a tool for companies not individuals. It was not until the mid-1990s—when Intel launched its first 32-bit Pentium processors and Microsoft launched 32-bit Windows NT—that

3D CAD first came within reach of small design shops, independent engineers, and students working from home.

On the software side, the breakthrough event came in 1995, when Boston-based SolidWorks (founded in 1993) launched SolidWorks 95, which was said to offer "80 percent of Pro/Engineer's functionality at 20 percent of the price." Two years later, SolidWorks was acquired by Dassault.

Meanwhile, in the mega-corporate arena, 3D CAD was subsumed into the broader category of product lifecycle management (PLM) systems. And in this field, the mid-1990s benchmark was Boeing's development of its 777 airliner in record time using a completely paperless system.

Since the millennium, the headline story has been consolidation as larger fish ate smaller ones to the point that only four whales survive: Dassault Systèmes, Autodesk, PTC, and Siemens PLM. After the frenzied developments of the 1980s and 1990s, so far this century has been relatively quiet. But just watch: The cloud is going to change that.

Today, though, 3D CAD is the indispensable tool for the world's elite mechanical engineers, designers, architects, and animators. Although prices have dropped over the years, serious software packages still start at around $4,000 per seat, plus an annual subscription fee for support and upgrades. You also need a computer with significant memory and compute power, along with a high-end graphics card. Cheap it's not, but the tools are now within reach of a serious freelancer, at least in the developed nations.

Although by now a commodity, 2D CAD remains a useful tool priced at levels you would expect to pay for any shrink-wrapped software, with programs priced similarly to anything else you might buy for your laptop.

All told, there are now nearly 20 million 2D and 3D CAD users around the world. But here is the key number to remember: Worldwide, there are still just 3.1 million licensed users of 3D CAD. This number is important because it clearly defines the size of the world's professional design elite.

Cloud Looms over the Picnic

Since the industry consolidated into four giant players, life has been like a sunny Sunday picnic for the survivors. Growth has been steady; margins have remained fat. As the song says, "fish are jumping and the cotton is high."

But in the past few years, a cloud has begun to loom over the party, and the happy picnickers have been unsure whether to move or hope it passes over. Actually, it's *the* cloud—cloud computing that threatens to disrupt the installed software business model. And the CAD makers are probably more vulnerable to the cloud than any other software sector.

In talking to a great many CAD users, the sense I get is that customers are generally happy with the tools themselves. They are impeccable and getting better all the time. The problem— and it's a significant obstacle—is the hoops that all four vendors make their customers jump through.

As a group, the four vendors have impressive pricing power over their customers. Buying a seat requires a significant up-front investment, and you don't have the opportunity to buy just one slice of pizza; you have to buy the whole package, even if you use it only once a month.

Why would any engineer use a platform just once a month? Didn't I just tell you that we lived in our CAD screens?

Each of the vendors has a proprietary system incompatible with all the others. And Dassault has two, CATIA and SolidWorks, that are still incompatible with each other. So if you are a parts supplier serving multiple original equipment manufacturers (OEMs), this incompatibility means that you may have to run several CAD platforms just to stay in the loop.

Incompatibility is designed to lock customers in, and it works. If you switch vendors, you effectively lose your entire CAD archive, because none of it will be usable on the new system. All this unnecessarily complicates any effort to merge two big companies, or even to form intercorporate research alliances, such as the green powertrain tie-ups that several automakers have initiated.

Clever as this strategy may have seemed, the vendors have shot themselves in the foot with it. After consolidating down to four giants, incompatibility effectively means further mergers and acquisitions (M&As) would be difficult. To learn more about the four giants, please see the Appendix.

Still basking in the glow of their hugely expanded design capability, customers were willing to put up with all this inconvenience and premium pricing—at least until recently. What's more, there seemed to be no alternative until, at almost the same moment, everyone noticed the cloud looming in the sky. And that was the exact moment when a random Estonian wandered into the picture.

I Looked up at the Cloud . . . and Saw the Ball Heading Straight at Me

The thrill of coming to America for some people may be the lottery ticket slim chance of bumping into Bob Dylan on a

New York street or seeing Scarlett Johansson sashay out of a Hollywood restaurant. For a CADomaniac like me, though, the thrill of coming to America was the possibility of meeting the stars of the CAD universe—people like Carl Bass.

Liken it to anything you want, you can't overstate how crucial CAD is to gearheads like me. For us, CAD is like the electric guitar for rockers, like the brush for a painter, or as I said before, like the horse to a cowboy. And also like I said, after a long week of driving a 3D CAD screen at work, many of us will come straight home and dive into our hobby projects. If not outright obsessed, we are least heavily CAD-involved.

So as I sat in a Boston café in November 2010 considering what to do a couple of weeks later when I would reach San Francisco, I wasn't thinking about how to meet Steve Jobs. Another luminary from across the Golden Gate in Marin County was on my mind: Carl Bass, the president and CEO of Autodesk, the number two player in CAD. From what I had read, he sounded like an innovator and a visionary, and I was eager to meet him.

In a company as big as Autodesk, though, you can't just wander into the CEO's waiting room and sit down to wait for your turn to see the boss. So I sat in the café surfing the Internet and trying to think of some way to get face time with Carl.

That's when I came across a notice about Autodesk University, the giant extravaganza that the CAD maker puts on every year, drawing thousands of users from around the world. As I read about the three-day event it sounded like a CAD Woodstock—maybe CADstock. I was almost too excited when I found it was at the beginning of December—in Las Vegas!—just when I was supposed to fly to San Francisco. Surely I could change my ticket to get Vegas as a stopover.

Then, suddenly, my enthusiasm hit the wall of cold, hard reality. To attend Autodesk University would cost me $2,000—much more than all the money I had left. But my hopes soared again minutes later after a friend came in and heard my sad tale.

"That's an easy hurdle to jump," he said. "All you have to do is contact their PR department and tell them you're a journalist from Estonia. Tell them you're from any newspaper you like—they won't phone all the way over there to check."

So that's what I did. And bless the people on the media relations team at Autodesk who accepted my bogus claim at face value: They gave me the press pass I needed, and I flew to Las Vegas.

Maybe it's because of our history, but most Estonians don't expect their luck to be good, which is why we're not big on casinos. Luck was with me when I arrived in Vegas to register for the big event, though. When they saw that I was (supposedly) a journalist, the desk staff informed me that I was invited to a media roundtable the next morning, December 2. There would be just 20 reporters there, talking with . . . *ka-ching* . . . Carl Bass.

All through the roundtable my mind raced as I tried to focus on what I wanted to say and struggled to summon up the English vocabulary with which to say it. At the end of the event I got my chance, so I sidled up to the front as nonchalantly as I could.

Next thing I knew, there was Carl's hand thrust out to shake mine. I wish I had a video of the elevator pitch I made to him then. As awkward as it felt to me, I must have said something that caught his attention . . . because his immediate response was, "Come and see me tomorrow at my office in San Francisco."

Actually, I knew the pitch by heart, because it was the story I had been telling over and over for two months since arriving in America:

> CAD is going to the cloud, because the cloud is going to give engineers access to more sophisticated tools that require massive processing power. And the cloud is going to be neutral—software agnostic—making it easier for engineers to collaborate remotely, with no more worries about incompatibility. So the installed software model is doomed.
>
> If engineers are going to access the cloud from a neutral platform, that's not going to be some CAD vendor's portal. It's going to be social media, a platform that creates a sense of community and a critical mass of collective knowledge. The tools are going to be accessed from a place where the users feel at home. And that place is the cloud, because the cloud is open—and that openness is critical.
>
> So when you're developing cloud software, you want to make sure that the underlying functionality, the API, is built so that it's easily accessible from different environments—both Web and mobile. That also makes integration with other applications really easy. So when you translate this to CAD, it's going to change everything. Imagine if every item in the CAD system could be easily accessible anywhere: the geometry, the materials, the part numbers. That opens up tremendous opportunities. Different software vendors tend be obsessively focused on solving very specific problems, and they don't need to be limited by the paradigm inside the CAD system. And because all of these tools are built in an open environment, every tool will be specifically built to perform one task, and they will all talk to each other in a seamless way . . .

Or something like that. I must have talked Carl's ear off, but as he says (see the next feature on Carl Bass), somehow I reminded him of himself when he was my age. Thank Heavens!

That night I flew to San Francisco and checked into a cheap hotel on Lombard Street, where I paced up and down working out what to say the next morning.

First thing, I made my way down to the foot of Market Street, near the Embarcadero, where Autodesk has a large office. After announcing myself at reception, I marveled at the gallery in Autodesk's lobby as I waited for Carl's assistant to come get me.

Soon I was ushered into a second-floor conference room, and before long, Carl strode in. The meeting didn't last long, maybe 20 minutes, but Carl listened attentively to what I said and asked insightful questions.

Although no immediate result came from that very cordial first meeting with Carl, just getting a meeting was a sign that the ball was somehow coming my way. From that point, events moved with a lightning speed that happens only in America.

Not long after that encounter in San Francisco, I began to understand how a Boston Red Sox outfielder must feel—standing way out in the middle of nowhere—when he suddenly realizes, "Omigawd, the ball is coming my way." And everyone in the crowd realizes the same thing at the same moment.

Six months later, GrabCAD had $1 million of venture capital funding and I had (after monumental hassle) a visa to live in the United States and had an office in Boston.

Two and a half years later, in June 2013, Carl and I appeared on a joint webcast—CEO to CEO—announcing the agreement between our two companies to feature Autodesk's new cloud-based 3D CAD tools on GrabCAD's Workbench collaborative platform.

Only in America.

Carl Bass: Three-Dimensional Mensch

They say you never want to meet your heroes, but I guess that depends on who your heroes are. If it's a guy like Carl Bass, president and CEO of Autodesk, the CAD software maker based in San Rafael, California, I can tell you the experience is likely to be a real pleasure. In his native Brooklyn, Carl is what they would call a real mensch, the kind of down-to-earth person who you know would talk to the guy at the gas station with the same respect and empathy he shows to the CEO of Chevron.

So even if he doesn't recall it, I will never forget the sincere warmth I encountered when I approached Carl at a media event, a random Estonian with a lump in my throat, to give him my elevator pitch for my vision of CAD in the cloud. When interviewed by our research team for this book, Carl said all he remembers is that "every time I turned around to get a cup of coffee there was Hardi." Fortunately for me, this level of persistence reminded Carl of himself when he was my age.

In fact, Carl is so persistent that he may be the only guy ever to become CEO of a major company that fired him. His predecessor, Carol Bartz, had done just that in 1995, when she got fed up with Carl's continual nagging. To her great credit (and his), Bartz turned around and rehired him a few months later when colleagues said they couldn't do without him. When he took the helm at Autodesk in 2006, a profile by Carla Bova in the local Marin County newspaper quoted Bartz about her decision: "If he has enough to do, great, because if he doesn't have enough to do, he is a total pain in the ass."

The same article goes on to quote J. Hallam Dawson, an Autodesk board member, about the process of getting Carl from his rehiring to his desk in the C-suite. "We actually got Carl to the point where he has a suit. He used to wander around in Birkenstocks. He was a classic technology guy who did not care about how he looked or what he wore. He was just fascinated with technology," Dawson said. "He has grown a lot since then, but at heart that is where he is. He walks around with no pretension."

Lack of pretension never got anyone to the corner office, though. What got Carl to the top, in my opinion, is a farsighted vision of where CAD is going, grounded in deep knowledge of the fundamentals. So we asked Carl what he sees over the horizon.

GrabCAD: The conversation started with Hardi telling you where *he* thought the cloud is going to take CAD. Where do *you* think the cloud revolution is going to take CAD?

Carl Bass: As with every revolution, new winners will emerge as technologies and business models transition. It is unlikely that the current leaders will be the leaders of the future. At Autodesk, we stuck our neck out because

(continued)

(continued)

we saw the future potential of a cloud-based platform that combined mobile with a social environment that enables collaboration. We created cloud-based PLM, then added Simulation and now industrial and mechanical design with Fusion 360—a complete portfolio in the cloud.

There is a huge cultural shift happening. People are being given better tools, and the changes these tools are facilitating are unprecedented. With change comes challenge, but then the new tools come along and the things we have been trying to solve and the capabilities we have been trying to offer our customers are suddenly easier. Collaboration was different before. Now collaboration has changed forever, and the problem of delivering this to our customers has become much simpler. With changes in technology, problems simplify and the technology then changes the context of our industry.

Our focus is on what tools to provide. The questions have become: What do our customers want to do? What is possible now? What can we provide with the current technology, and what will we be able to provide in the future?

GrabCAD: In this book, Hardi is exploring the changes
               taking place as engineers and designers
               get access to phenomenally powerful new
               tools and discover new ways to collaborate.
               Where is this going to lead in terms of
               innovation?

Carl Bass: Small, agile companies now have unprec-
               edented ability to compete. The cost of
               start-ups is decreasing . . . and we see
               an unprecedented availability of capi-
               tal through entities like Angel List and
               Kickstarter. This comes just as we have a
               convergence of new materials and processes
               across the spectrum. Plus, we have this
               utterly brand new ability to use these pow-
               erful tools in collaboration with others via
               the cloud.

               So I've been saying that innovation is
               happening at an unprecedented pace and it's
               going to continue to accelerate because of
               five trends: (1) the move from owning prod-
               ucts to accessing experiences; (2) changes
               in the way companies do business, with
               developments like the cloud and crowd
               sourcing; (3) digital fabrication that changes
               the rules of how things are made; (4) the
               rise of information . . . and the vast amount
               of information now available to us; and

               (continued)

(continued)

(5) the fact that computing power is becoming infinite, ubiquitous, and virtually free.

GrabCAD: There's a perception out there that Autodesk is stronger in civil engineering and architecture than in mechanical. Now that your cloud-based tools are available through GrabCAD, mechanical engineers and industrial designers are getting a chance to see what Autodesk offers. How significant and strategic is this for your business?

Carl Bass: Autodesk is best known by what our customers do. Just today, I was walking through our Autodesk Gallery and overheard a group of departing visitors say the same thing I've heard said many times: "I had no idea that Autodesk did this." People in the film industry think that we do one thing. Architects think we do another. Mechanical engineers and industrial designers think we do something entirely different. Everyone sees us through a particular lens. We are a billion-dollar business, and far broader than most know.

As for our partnership with GrabCAD, we're in the early days and we are really excited about the future. Hardi has built a great, vast, and vibrant community of users.

And we have the best cloud-based portfolio of tools in the world. . . . I feel that everyone is just beginning to understand the possibilities.

People don't understand how influenced and restricted they can be by a particular mind-set. I feel that Autodesk and GrabCAD are breaking down old barriers and beginning to redefine the way people interact and work. With the people and the tools available today, we can accomplish almost anything.

I would have to agree with Carl on that. And the key to what we can accomplish is collaboration, among engineers and their colleagues and among the four giant CAD vendors: Dassault Systèmes, Autodesk, PTC, and Siemens.

As a leader in the CAD industry, Carl is unique in a great many ways . . . but CAD users should be encouraged to hear that he is far from the only really smart and immensely likable person at the top of the industry. Of course you find all types, but for me it has been a great experience to meet the leaders of all the major vendors—people such as Mike Payne, Steven Walski, Jon Hirstick, and Jeff Ray—and I look forward to working with all of them. But Carl gets profiled here because he was the first to open his door to me.

Executive Takeaways

- In software, cloud computing is going to disrupt business models across the board. For many companies, the dilemma is whether to preserve existing business or shoot for new customers who will embrace the new wave. How can you adapt to the new without losing what you have?

- What's the next wave in your space? Is there a trend that your younger employees are all over but that your senior people see as a waste of time?

- What are you doing to keep an eye on the new ideas that aren't yet prevalent today but might be tomorrow?

3 A Million Engineers on the March

When I got my U.S. work visa and moved to Boston in June 2011, the GrabCAD community was still a small town: population 6,405 on the first day of that month. Thirty months later, in December 2013, we were a thriving metropolis with a population that had just passed the one million mark. It's an active and intense community: Each month members upload more than 50,000 three-dimensional computer-aided design (3D CAD) files to the site and post 30,000-plus comments.

In social media terms, okay, one million users is peanuts. But ours is not a community of random chatter; virtually all members are users of 3D CAD, which distinguishes them as members of the world's engineering and design elite. How can we tell they use 3D CAD? Because they have taken the trouble to download one or more 3D CAD files posted by their peers, files that are useless unless you have 3D CAD and know how to use it.

This is the real measure of our community's magnitude. Worldwide there are 3.1 million licensed users of 3D CAD; nearly one-third of them are now members of the GrabCAD community.

This is why I'm going to talk quite a bit about GrabCAD in this chapter—not to promote the company (though I'm sure you'll understand my enthusiasm) but because the growth of our community demonstrates the central message of this book—that the process and culture of engineering is changing.

The real significance of our community is that it's proving to be amazingly fertile ground for the organic growth and evolution of what we call open engineering. Although to be fair, it's not just about engineering; it's about the convergence of engineering with design, manufacturing, marketing, and more.

It is also about the search for new flexible ways to bring greater inspiration, craft skill, quality execution, and market awareness to the process of developing physical goods. Even more, it's about engineers and designers evolving their own ways to learn and work, beyond the top-down framework of corporate priorities and engineering school curricula.

It's about engineers and designers running their own show.

That's why we don't pretend to *own* these million users. They pay nothing to join the community or use our site. Nor do we sell them to advertisers. You won't find a single ad on our site. As hosts of the community, we provide a conducive environment and some ground rules. In fact, we have taken great care not to act like the police, instead letting the community itself decide where it wants to go.

We don't aim to be a nonprofit, of course. But where we hope to make money is through providing pay-as-you-go tools on our platform that members can use, or not. It's their choice with absolutely no coercion.

What's more, we can hardly claim that the shape and scope of our community is the result of some grand design. More than anything, it is a product of serendipity.

We Set Out to Stop Reinventing the Wheel . . . and Ended up with Something Unexpected

My original idea, way back in Tallinn in 2008, was to create an online CAD service bureau. Customers would bring us their needs; we would make money by finding engineers to meet those needs. The trick was, how could we attract engineers to do the work? We needed some sort of social magnet—but what?

On another track in my thinking was something that had bothered me for a long time. Each time we set out to design something in CAD, we had to start from scratch, which meant that we had to continually, and quite literally, reinvent the wheel—the epitome of wasted effort that is embedded in every language. Since I had one foot in mechanical engineering and the other in software, this was too ridiculous to ignore. In information technology (IT), it's standard practice to use open source code or ready-made components wherever possible. But for 3D CAD, there was not a lot available.

Gradually, the two questions fused in my mind. How do we create a CAD toolbox, and how do we become a social magnet for CAD? From there, the answer seemed obvious: Why not create an open source platform where people could share their CAD files?

To find the answer, we floated the idea past 10 mechanical engineers, and every single one responded, "No way anybody is going to share files. Forget about it." Open source might be standard practice in software, but in the highly patent-conscious world of physical design, everyone said that sharing CAD files would never fly.

If I'd been diligent and earned an MBA before attempting to go into business, maybe I would have realized that you are supposed to "respect the process" and base every move on carefully conducted research. Being too young, uneducated, and stubborn to know better, however, I said, "Screw the research; we're just going to do it!"

When we finally added a CAD file-sharing function to the GrabCAD site in August 2010, it was like skinny-dipping; no one wanted to go first. Everyone wanted to download and take a peek at what others had, but no one wanted to upload their own content.

At first it seemed the skeptics were right, but by that point we just couldn't admit defeat. So we uploaded every CAD file we had ever made and strong-armed every engineer we knew into uploading their own files. It took a while, but eventually we reached a tipping point where people could see that everyone else was doing it, and they began to join in.

Having discovered they could download ingenious devices and see the design tricks behind them, CADomaniac engineers were fascinated. And when they began to see how much interest was generated by items shared on the site, shyness shifted to exhibitionism, or something like it. Before long, people were eager to show the world what they could do.

For some it was the glow of kudos that comes when the community "likes" their designs. For others it was learning from constructive criticism or tips, as in "That's cool, but if you added fins, stability would improve."

Such observations sparked a huge volume of intense discussion on highly specific technical topics. As a result, it was not long before anyone scouring the Web on these subjects was sure to get search results pointing to a CAD file or a discussion on our site. Try searching for any mechanical device you like, plus "CAD." Chances are that GrabCAD will appear on the top page of results.

Once through our door, it is a rare CADomaniac who is not amazed by the treasure trove to be found inside. Every day we receive e-mails from people who are so excited you might think they had stumbled on the Lost City of the Incas. These love letters make my day.

Three years after our initial launch, we have an archive of more than 400,000 CAD projects. How do our members use them?

The house rule is that you are free to make noncommercial use of any file you download. As long as you don't out-and-out copy a design, you can use what you learn from studying it in your own commercial work. As my engineer friend Andy Payne says, "Sometimes it's just useful to see how other designers have overcome the obstacles you face."

Often that results in downloaders contacting the originator to ask for advice, which sometimes leads to an offer to license the design or even commissioning the originator to adapt it.

So, yes, literally, our community eliminates the need to reinvent the wheel. On GrabCAD you will find wheels for cars, trucks, off-road vehicles, wheelbarrows, furniture, bicycles, tricycles, skateboards, and trams. Plus you'll find suspensions, axles, bearings, and accessories such as a device for changing bike tires. Detailed plans for anything and everything to do with the wheel are there, ready to be downloaded.

If you are into, say, designing mountain bikes and your main interest is the frame or the gearing, the ability to download a wheel and use it straight away is a boon. Because no matter how fantastic your frame might be, it's useless without wheels—and there's no sense in reinventing them.

A lot of the time, though, community members have no intention of actually making the designs they download. For those who are into 3D CAD, the design details in a well-made

CAD file are endlessly fascinating—and that's what makes an online CAD archive so magnetic.

What fascinates me is how our members are evolving the community. I could ramble on for page after page trying to explain what our members are working toward and what it means to them, but there is no substitute for the authentic experience of real people. So I'll let Verislav Mudrak, William Barclay, Venkatasubramanian, Tommy Mueller, Terry Stonehocker, Andreas Gkertsos, Chris Shakal, and Sasank Gopinathan speak for themselves. (If you're wondering why I've listed in this wonderful collection of names in this order, read on to learn about GrabCAD score. Verislav definitely tops the list.)

Four Flywheels Driving Open Engineering

1. A New Marketplace for Engineering Talent

When evaluating a candidate for a technical job, sure, it's good to know which engineering school his parents paid for or who has hired her before. But to my mind it's much more useful to see what an engineer can actually *do* and how much respect peers have for that work.

In the GrabCAD community, talent stands out. Look up any member and you will find his or her biography, listing work and educational history, interests, skills, equipment, and location on the planet. What you will also see is a portfolio of design projects and renderings, any of which you can download and examine in minute detail.

Plus, you see a table of statistics (engineers love quantifying things) showing how many times people have viewed their profile, how many times people have downloaded or commented on their CAD files, and what their GrabCAD score is.

The score for each member is generated by our algorithm that essentially rewards involvement in the community: contributing CAD files is good; helping other community members is great. Perhaps the best reward is that the default listing of our members puts the highest scorer at the top. Along with the merit badges we give out, the score is an incentive to good citizenship.

Of course, many of the best engineers are too busy to put enough effort into the community to rack up a high score. So the best way to learn who's really got the goods is to download their designs and see for yourself. Or you can see what comments peers have left and how many times a file has been downloaded.

The net effect is very tangible street cred for talented engineers and designers—and a playing field that puts MIT grads on the same level as those of us with degrees from Tallinna University of Technology. It's about what you can actually do.

Even after just two years, we can see the development a new marketplace for engineering and design talent that is opening a world of opportunity for professionals with outstanding CAD skills.

Suddenly, in small-town South Carolina, Terry Stonehocker (http://grabcad.com/terry.stonehocker), 58 and jobless, gets commissions from California. In the depths of Greece's economic meltdown, out of the blue Andreas Gkertsos (http://grabcad.com/andreas.gkertsos) gets a great job offer. Out in Oregon, self-taught Tommy Mueller (http://grabcad.com/ tommy.mueller-1) finds Hollywood asking for his help. And way over in Cochin, India, Sasank Gopinathan (http://grabcad .com/sasank.gopinathan) becomes the go-to guy for an American maker of supercars.

It's a new business model that works for both sides.

The world's most savvy buyers of design and engineering skill are catching on. Senior corporate engineers now sift through the ranks of our community, instead of relying on human resources to go through a stack of résumés (that weird, stilted, and archaic document format) to select what they think an engineer should look like. Rather than hiring blind, they are discovering the wisdom of opening the windows to fresh insight and giving external talent the opportunity to show what value they can add. It's a path that may lead to full-time employment or just an ongoing outsource relationship.

Companies such as GE and Nokia are beginning to jump in with both feet, issuing open "Challenges" to our community. Companies post a spec describing a puzzle that needs solving. They then appoint a panel of judges (usually a mix of their people and GrabCAD staff) to judge the most ingenious solutions proposed, which is rewarded with prize money.

Our Challenge page is great fun for engineers, who love nothing more than a puzzle. So tens of thousands typically visit each month—and a surprising number find a challenge that makes them say, "I bet I could do that." As you will read in Chapter 5, GE was absolutely amazed by the sophistication of nearly 700 responses to its recent challenge.

What Is a Challenge?

It turns out that a million minds are better than one.
Or at least that's the lesson from our Challenges, where
companies ask our million members to help them solve
their hardest engineering problems. The sponsor identifies
a particular problem, such as an old part that has never
worked quite right, an aesthetic challenge they'd like
the design world's opinion on, or a desire to inject some
fresh ideas into their current in-house design department.
Next they create a contest around that problem and, with
our help, post it to our community. Finally, the sponsor selects their top choices from the entrants. Winners
get cash prizes, gifts, and a chance to test their skills and
occasionally land a dream job, while the sponsor gets creativity, fresh thinking, and "elastic" engineering resources.
Everyone wins.

2. A Powerful Social Magnet

Designing and building physical products is an inherently social
activity: It usually takes a team with diverse skills to get the job
done. However, it's a social activity undertaken by people who
typically are not all that social. We tend to be doers not talkers.
On the weekend we're happiest tinkering away by ourselves in
the garage. Yes, many of us do have a fondness for beer, but at
parties, ordinary people's eyes usually glaze over if we start talking about what we do.

The truth is that becoming a mechanical engineer doesn't enhance your sex appeal. We don't have the kind of glamour (or wealth) bestowed on programmers in Silicon Valley. Dilbert is a sex god by comparison. We don't get much respect, and what respect we do get usually comes from working for big companies, which is a natural habitat for us given that large automakers and aerospace companies hire mechanical engineers in 10,000 lots. So people nod approvingly when you say, "I work for Boeing," or "I work for Ford."

Perhaps the luckiest engineers are those who live in places such as Boston, across the street from MIT (as I do now), or near Caltech in Southern California. These places offer engineers vibrant physical communities and plenty of intellectual stimulation, not to mention the job opportunities from new ventures that spin off from major engineering schools.

I was lucky to come of age in post-Soviet Tallinn, where there was a certain excitement around engineering, even if it was ultimately not enough to satisfy me. So I really have empathy for those who live in places without a lot of engineering activity—or, even worse, places such as Michigan, where engineering has dwindled as manufacturing moved offshore.

This is not to imply that we are a bunch of lonely heart losers, just that something has been missing in our lives. Too many of us have been isolated, and too often, our self-esteem has come more from the brands we work for rather than the recognition of our achievements by people who could actually understand their value, namely our peers.

It's a hole that *Popular Mechanics* once helped paper over in an abstract, passive kind of way. We could read about what was happening in our field and get a glimpse of it. Online forums have come closer to addressing it, in that they give us a chance to talk *about* the work. But it's only *about* the work; it's not the work itself.

What has happened with putting our work in CAD and sharing it over the Internet is that the experience is no longer abstract or passive. In a very real sense we've gained the ability to share the work itself in a way that allows us to take it apart, to see how it's made, and to discuss it on a very hands-on informed level.

This is a very powerful magnet that is making people who were never all that social suddenly highly social. We have something to talk about that is highly compelling, and we have the means to talk about it.

At GrabCAD, all we did was put out a petri dish with a medium in which this culture could grow. Ever since, when we come to the office each morning we are blown away to see how it has grown overnight.

Beyond just its propensity to multiply, what is really rewarding to see in our community's culture is how remarkably warmhearted and supportive it has become on its own—and how global: My staff tell me we have members in 217 countries. But there aren't that many countries, are there? Still, even discounting those who falsely claim to live on Norfolk Island, we can see real members in all sorts of unlikely places.

Sure, we have our trolls, flamers, and chronic complainers, but when they get out of hand, it's usually the community itself that discourages their uncivil behavior. We set the tone from the beginning, but there was no "Voice of God" handing down Ten Commandments. Today, we rarely have to intervene.

You might be taking a risk letting engineers loose in a sculpture gallery or an art museum, given how fond we are of taking things apart just to see how they fit together. But in our art gallery, with its vast collection of 3D sculpture, that's half the fun.

Browse through the 400,000 CAD projects on our site and tell me what you see is not art. I would say that CAD has given rise to a remarkable flowering of artistic talent that our community has cultivated.

For the most part, mechanical engineers used to focus narrowly on function and leave whatever aesthetic touches to the designers. What we see now is that even with factory machines, our engineers take great care to make them look attractive in elaborate renderings—all the more so when they know their works will be viewed with interest by an informed audience.

Much more than simply admiring each other's work, there is a strong emphasis on spontaneously helping fellow members overcome technical hurdles and improve their designs.

3. A New Model of Engineering Education

From the outset, GrabCAD was intended to help engineers find work—that was what I was looking for myself. What I never anticipated was how the community would evolve, of its own accord, into a de facto educational institution that some members say is "better than any engineering school."

Maybe it's because 3D CAD is still relatively new, but learning how to use it is not yet at the core of many mechanical engineering curricula. In fact, a lot of veteran professors don't even know how to use it. In many cases, training programs offered by the software makers themselves are not much better.

That leaves many engineering undergraduates struggling to learn on their own. In the process, more than a few happen upon the GrabCAD site.

When Venkatasubramanian (http://grabcad.com/venkatasubramanian) discovered GrabCAD in 2011 as an undergrad in India, he says he was at first intimidated by the sophistication of the models he found. So was William Barclay (http://grabcad.com/william-1) in Scotland at around the same time. But once they found the courage to step up and ask questions, both were astounded by the help they received from skilled members of the community.

"As a new member of the community, so many people helped me. I can still tell you every single name of the people who helped me out," William says.

Asking questions is the critical step, because until you do, no one knows you're lurking in the background. Once you take that step, however, mentors typically respond with useful advice. Often that starts with a suggestion to download a certain CAD model and see how its designer handled the issue in question.

Once the novice has something to show, experienced hands will download his or her file and offer constructive criticism. Chris Shakal (http://grabcad.com/chris.shakal), an aspiring aircraft engine designer in Florida, credits expert members' critiquing of his early efforts with his quick mastery of CAD. "Even during freshman year, I had fourth-year engineering students asking me for help with their CATIA homework," he says.

Even better is what happens when someone asks a really good question. In response, members often put incredible effort—working an entire weekend gratis—into creating step-by-step tutorials on how to create various features in CAD. We now have thousands of these on file.

So what's emerging is a new and different type of engineering school: a lifelong, peer-to-peer learning culture, an environment in which students quickly become teachers.

It's already happening. It seems like 5 minutes ago that young William was the shy new lad in the class. Now he's an absolute ace at rendering, a true artist, and our most prolific producer of tutorials. There he is in Glasgow, the birthplace of modern mechanical engineering but sadly now the heart of Scotland's rust belt. I'll bet on him and his mates to lead Scotland back to its rightful place at the top of the league in engineering.

I have to take a deep breath every time I try to say his name, but Venkatasubramanian has already embarked on a promising career in software. And his name is up in large type on our office wall, underneath a huge mural of his radial engine design. If not for GrabCAD he says, "I think I would have become an eccentric, rustic person that speaks pathetic English with no passion toward anything."

India produces an impressive number of engineering graduates, but it's tough to get a place in one of the nation's top engineering school—especially if you come from an out-of-the-way place. So it's really gratifying to watch guys such as Venkatasubramanian and Sasank Gopinathan develop their own skills with the help of the GrabCAD community.

Down near Cape Canaveral, meanwhile, Chris Shakal, an undergraduate, is already getting offers from the aerospace industry. Watch; he's going to help America get wherever it wants to go in the solar system.

For these kids, GrabCAD is already the alma mater, and we're hardly three years old. But unlike previous generations that have emerged for conventional engineering schools, they are not going to graduate and go away. Many will stay because from here on this is where a lot of us are going to work.

4. A New Workplace in the Cloud

Whether they work at home or an office somewhere, many of our members now have a window into the community always open in their toolbar. Just like someone in a brick-and-mortar office peaking above the cubicle divider and calling out, "Hey, anyone know where I can find a widget?" members are continually tossing questions back and forth. And designers are constantly diving into the archive to download components useful in their efforts. In a very real sense, this is now where we work.

With one million members, it's no longer a small town, of course. Myriad personal networks now link people with shared interests, be it a common language, a passion for aerodynamics, or an address in the same city. In addition, all sorts of ad hoc teams are forming—my favorite being our odd couple: Tommy Mueller in Oregon and Verislav Mudrak (http://grabcad.com/ verislav.mudrak) in Serbia (see the feature that follows).

Our independent engineers function almost like a medieval guild. If one person is overwhelmed with work, he or she will pass the overflow to a trusted fellow member. Or if part of a project is outside one person's competence, that person may sub it out to the member "who really knows." And in our community you can easily find out which person really knows.

The next step, already under way, is to provide tools right inside the community that allow members to collaborate seamlessly with one another and with external clients. When I say "inside the community," I mean that's where the portal is; the tools themselves are in the cloud.

Workbench, our proprietary collaboration tool, is just what its name suggests: a platform on which 3D CAD projects sit as they are being built. It's a virtual platform located in a secure space, a workshop in the cloud. In this space, 3D models can be edited just using a Web browser, and they can be shared instantly. With complete control of the workshop keys, the project's owner can give access to whoever needs to be in all or part of it, one subcontractor or an entire group of clients. In fact, the workshop is so spacious that 10,000 customers can fit inside for a demonstration.

Bottom Line: This Revolution Is Bottom Up

A revolution is in progress as technological innovation creates vast new potential to unleash human ingenuity in the design and development of physical objects. But it's not being driven by software makers or large engineering firms or some futurist guru; it's happening before my eyes, although I'm certainly not leading it.

It is the collective will and wisdom of one million engineers and designers that drives this revolution forward. Something magical is happening as a new "culture of making things" coalesces.

New modes of collaboration are emerging. Ad hoc project teams are coming together overnight in order to swarm challenges that demand a variety of skill sets. Geographic barriers are disappearing as people reach across the globe to find the right expertise.

None of this would be possible without the informed trust that comes from high-bandwidth social interaction and being able to transparently see what others can achieve with CAD.

What's really exciting is that this new culture of open engineering—as I like to call it—is about to converge with a new generation of tools that support close collaboration in an open environment. It's a combination that promises to radically reorder the way physical objects are imagined and engineered.

Meet the Engineers at the Forefront . . .

As a new era of open engineering emerges, the lives and career paths of individual engineers all around the world are changing—for the better. Here are some of the talented people discovering new ways to find work, to learn, and to collaborate.

Terry Stonehocker

Member since November 2010

GrabCAD score: 9,568

"I ran into the 'no job thing' in late 2010, when the economy took a nosedive here, and I was about to go out of my mind when by accident I found GrabCAD," Terry Stonehocker recalls. "At the time, I had no idea what GrabCAD would do for me. I was 58 years old, living in small-town South Carolina, and I'd been self-employed for about 15 years. So finding a job in the corporate world again just was not happening."

(continued)

(*continued*)

In such a scenario, it is hard to argue that the odds of success for Terry were anything other than dismal, measurable only in nano-units. And that's why I treasure his story.

When he joined GrabCAD, Terry was in the middle of working on a model of a Bobber motorcycle, "to keep myself from going crazy," as he says. When the model was complete, he uploaded it to our site.

"Next thing I knew, people from all over the world were contacting me, telling me what a great job I'd done on the model," Terry says. "This got me pumped."

What Terry's woeful self-description omits is the undeniable fact that he is one deeply skilled dude. His background includes machine design, machine building, 3D modeling, patents filed, CNC programming, and graphic design. Plus, he has a passion for motorcycles that runs deep.

"When I was in high school back in the late 1960s in Germany [his father was serving in the U.S. Forces there], I fell in love with the BSA Motorcycle. When I came back to the States and started college, I got my first motorcycle, a Honda 305 Dream. The movie *Easy Rider* came out and the chopper craze was on. The rest is history."

He set out to be an architect in college, but he got thrown off that path by his passion for engineering. "I soon realized that I missed tinkering with gizmos and decided to change my major to mechanical engineering," he says.

As a mechanical engineer, Terry developed the first ever no-down-tube trike and won first place in the Daytona Rat's Hole custom bike show. His Gear Gasm custom bikes are among the most distinctive motorcycles on the planet. But eventually, as he says, Terry fell on hard times.

This changed once he joined the GrabCAD community and, as he puts it, "got pumped." Terry quickly started to get his mojo back.

"I started a new project drawing an old 1952 Harley Davidson FL motorcycle," he says. "I drew the panhead drivetrain first and uploaded it. That got me more attention, and then I got an e-mail from Hardi asking me if I'd be interested in working on some projects for GrabCAD. I replied with great excitement and told him that I would love to. That was when it all started for me, things just started falling into place, and the next thing I know I am covered up with work to do and so many new friends all over the world."

Terry also became part of a group of community members that helped to guide the site's development and shape many of its key features. "I was humbled by the expertise and talent of the individuals in this group," he says.

Even though he has hit 60, Terry now looks to the future, not the past. In addition to designing custom motorcycles, he has gone back to college. All the while he looks forward to collaborating with engineers from around the world.

(continued)

(continued)

"We have a lot of great minds in the community," Terry says, "and GrabCAD has the vision to put together the tools that will bring us together and unleash a new wave of engineering potential. I am indeed looking forward to the future, and it is looking very promising."

Andreas Gkertsos

Member since September 2011

GrabCAD score: 7,213

If Terry thought he had it tough in South Carolina, these days there is probably no tougher job market than Greece, where Andreas Gkertsos managed to snag a great position without going abroad . . . thanks to his achievements in the GrabCAD community.

Growing up in Athens as the son of a mechanic who specialized in outboard motors, Andreas's father encouraged him to follow in his footsteps. Andreas had other ideas: "I knew what I wanted. My dream was to become a good mechanical engineer and designer."

In 2011, he was a sophomore mechanical engineering student in a four-year program at the Technological Educational Institute of Piraeus, the port of Athens. And it was while searching the Web for CAD models that Andreas first noticed GrabCAD.

"At that point, most of my knowledge of SolidWorks came from resellers' training programs," he recalls. "When I would search the Internet, I noticed that GrabCAD was always among the top answers on Google. From the very beginning, the site was remarkable to me. The comments, the questions and answers, the models . . . it didn't take long to realize that there was a lot of truly professional work on GrabCAD. I decided right away to join the community, and I have not looked back since."

Andreas began by uploading models to GrabCAD and soliciting feedback from the community. At first, his models were quite simple, but with advice and support from his peers, his confidence and skills began to grow.

"You upload designs and receive feedback, and you comment on other people's designs. This collaboration was unbelievable to me," Andreas says. He also found tremendous lessons in finished projects on the site, especially the precisely detailed mechanical parameters. "Access to these finished models was incredible. It's one of the best ways to learn and benefit from the talents and knowledge of others."

It wasn't long before Andreas made GrabCAD his default page. "I was all of a sudden part of a unique community, a group of people helping and competing, challenging one another." After about eight months, Andreas found that his CAD skills just exploded. "It is one thing to make a good looking picture, but design is much more than that. Through GrabCAD I began to build mechanical parameters into the design. It was only then that I began to feel like a mechanical designer."

By the third year of his program, Andreas found he was the only one in his class who knew 3D CAD, and his lead in skills was widening through participation in the community. "Participating in GrabCAD competitions helped me

(continued)

(*continued*)

focus," he says. "The competitions sharpen your skills, and the tutorials are wonderful. Not only have I learned from them, but I've won two prizes for my own tutorials."

Not long before graduation, Andreas received a message via GrabCAD from an injection-molded parts manufacturer in a neighboring city. "Unbeknownst to me, this company that manufactures kitchen and bathroom hardware had been tracking my activities on GrabCAD for over a year. They asked me to come in for an interview. When I met them, they asked me to generate two designs, which were not challenging for me. Very quickly, I was offered a position as an industrial designer."

Over the past two years, through the depths of the Greek economic crisis, Andreas has had a good and steady job. "Now my father is unemployed, and I am able to support my family. This is remarkable given the situation here. Without GrabCAD, things would be very different for me."

Andreas, who remains active in the community, has this advice for fledgling designers: "You can follow your dream with GrabCAD, no matter where you live or how limited you think your opportunities may be. I can say with confidence that I became a good designer because of GrabCAD."

Chris Shakal

Member since January 2012

GrabCAD score: 5,383

A Kansan and the son of an engineer, Chris Shakal is an aerospace engineering major at Embry-Riddle

Aeronautical University in Daytona Beach, Florida, not so far from the renowned Kennedy Space Center at Cape Canaveral. It's a program that has allowed him to bring his longtime aeronautical dreams to life in 3D CAD . . . ever since he joined the GrabCAD community in the middle of his freshman year.

He was introduced to CATIA V5 in an introductory drafting and CAD class in his first semester. "That was my first experience with any kind of CAD software. I have been really into it ever since. It's the ultimate combination of engineering and art—virtual LEGO," he says.

Even as a kid, Chris was designing his own creations, "from airplanes and trucks to a one-cylinder piston engine. But what I was really obsessed with was airplanes. I decided early on that I wanted a career in the aerospace industry."

He stumbled on GrabCAD while working on a jet engine model. "I was looking on Google for models of similar engines and found a nice rendering on GrabCAD. I poked around the rest of the site and couldn't believe something this awesome existed . . . the models, the tutorials."

Modeling airplanes and engines are still his passion, and he says that most of his models are his own designs, although a few are replicas ("as exact as I can make them") of classic designs like the Space Shuttle. "My models require plenty of reference points to make

(continued)

(continued)

sure the designs are fundamentally sound," he adds earnestly.

Thanks to support from the community, his skills have rocketed ahead to the point that he now makes tutorials as well as studying ones made by his peers. "So far, I've made tutorials for jet engine fans, jet engine exhaust mixers, and an entire jet engine," he says. "I've gotten plenty of positive feedback on them, and I plan on contributing more in the future."

Chris credits GrabCAD for enriching his CAD studies and motivating him to continue creating models long after his introductory CAD class ended. By creating models in CATIA, he says his skills, especially in surfacing, have markedly improved, and his progress has not gone unnoticed. "Even during freshman year, I had seniors asking me for help with their CATIA homework."

His current challenge is to teach himself rendering. "It's something I would really like to get down, because I've seen on GrabCAD how a good rendering can really make a model stand out."

So far, though, Chris has had no problem in getting his design portfolio to stand out on GrabCAD. Three of the top five most downloaded jet-engine designs on the site are his, and he has had numerous requests from GrabCAD engineers to use his models in various applications. That has not made him complacent, however. "Pretty much anyone can see my uploads, and I've already gotten job offers as a CAD designer through GrabCAD.

So I'm pushing myself to keep improving my skills, specifically in CATIA," he says. This year he is keeping busy helping other students as a teaching assistant in the introductory drafting and CAD course at Embry-Riddle.

Chris says it's been a great experience to watch GrabCAD grow. "Since joining in 2012, I've continued to notice the site evolving and expanding its reach in the engineering world. Open engineering platforms like this will continue to foster product design and collaboration. It will be interesting to see where GrabCAD is five years from now."

For our part, we can't wait to see where Chris is five years from now.

Venkatasubramanian

Member since September 2011

GrabCAD score: 12,113

When he discovered GrabCAD as a student at age 19, Venkatasubramanian never imagined that two years later he would be an associate software engineer with Accenture Services in Chennai, the city in southern India formerly known as Madras. "At that time I was new to CAD and studying Pro/Engineer," he says. "I was not at all confident that I would be able to do CAD very well."

Awestruck and intimidated by the quality of CAD models he found on the site, Venkatasubramanian marshaled the courage to download a few models and

(continued)

(*continued*)

challenge himself to learn CAD. This approach proved "very effective in gaining confidence, or what I like to call CAD-fidence," he quips "More important, GrabCAD was instrumental in helping me identify my passion for CAD."

He credits GrabCAD with helping him focus his efforts and energies on becoming a designer. "My radial engine model was a turning point in my CAD development. It was the first big and complex model that I succeeded with." Today, that radial engine model is an unmistakable feature of the décor at GrabCAD's head office in Cambridge, Massachusetts: a large-format mural with Venkatasubramanian's name next to it.

He describes GrabCAD as a "virtual ocean of CAD knowledge," adding that, "even someone with minimal knowledge could become well versed in CAD through viewing GrabCAD tutorials."

The community has also proved invaluable as a networking resource for him. "I have befriended many designers and from there extended my network through sites likes Facebook and LinkedIn. GrabCAD was the foundation for all of these activities," he says.

Those networking efforts have paid off. "Quite a number of designers have hired me for a wide variety of freelance projects, from common household items to firearms, for clients in Europe, Russia, and the United States," he says. What's more, he credits GrabCAD with helping him secure his new job, the first full-time position in his career.

Best of all, he says: "If GrabCAD didn't exist, I think I would have become an eccentric, rustic person that speaks pathetic English with no passion toward anything. Without GrabCAD I wouldn't have been recognized by so many prominent designers around the world or been granted so many opportunities to work in my field."

Looking to the future, Venkatasubramanian says he plans to pursue a master's degree in design and continue his participation in the GrabCAD community. "Today and in the future, engineering will continue to find itself in everything. Thanks to GrabCAD, I will be a part of this exciting future. We designers owe GrabCAD a lot."

William Barclay

Member since June 2011

GrabCAD score: 25,038

In the nineteenth century, Glasgow could fairly claim to be the Hollywood of mechanical engineering. More recently, and sadly, it has been the epicenter of Scotland's rust belt. But young William Barclay is proof that the city is still forging world-class engineers.

Then a novice at Motherwell College, on the fringe of his native city, William first encountered GrabCAD while searching the Web for anything that might enhance his grasp of 3D CAD.

"I came across GrabCAD by mistake, you might say," William recalls. "I caught the GrabCAD bug that day, and I still have it."

(continued)

(*continued*)

He was instantly amazed by the array of detailed models he found and was delighted to find he could download them for free.

"I spent a lot of time watching from the sidelines," he says, "examining the models and wondering if I would ever be able to create models of such caliber myself. But the community welcomed me with open arms, and immediately I began learning from others."

We were very soon aware of his presence, because William would post questions almost every day. And he says they never went unanswered. As a result, we were able to watch his CAD skills grow exponentially in the months after he joined.

He has not forgotten the support he received: "As a new member of the community so many people helped me. I can still tell you every single name of the people who helped me out."

One of William's "GrabCAD legends" advised him to download models and carefully study how they were created. "This was a critical piece of advice. From there my skills began to go from strength to strength. And this is something I continue to do to this day."

At one point, 20 community members helped out with a key assignment. "One member posted a paper I had written, and others provided feedback that helped shape my project's concept and final design."

As his skill level began to soar, fellow students and teachers took notice. "I told them how so many people had helped me on GrabCAD." Although none of his teachers had then heard of GrabCAD, it wasn't long before both his classmates and instructors joined. "Since then, I've spread the word to the new starts every semester," he says.

William's GrabCAD experience has had a major impact on his career path. "I want to be not just the one making the models [but the one] thinking about the design," he says. That prompted him to go on from his technical training course to pursue a degree in mechanical engineering at Glasgow Nautical College.

Although he's lost count of the number of tutorials he's watched, William says he has posted "20 to 25, and I plan to continue to do more." He sees this as his way of giving back to the community that has given him so much. He has also hosted a weekly GrabCAD blog, sharing the top models posted each seven-day period. "I just love to watch someone new to CAD and see their talents grow from strength to strength."

Speaking of strength, William's own abilities have not gone unnoticed. "I've received many offers of employment, including three projects that I have completed . . . all from viewing my profile and contacting me through GrabCAD."

"GrabCAD has provided me with access to some of the top designers and engineers in the world," he says. "Just look at their profiles—it's down to that. This is a community and a collaborative environment unlike any other."

(continued)

(*continued*)

Sasank Gopinathan

Member since September 2011

GrabCAD score: 883

Sasank Gopinathan hails from Cochin in India's Kerala State. He describes himself as a "SolidWorks enthusiast and industrial designer by degree." In his heart, though, Sasank is an automotive designer. That might have been a problem because the southernmost tip of the subcontinent is a long, long way from Stuttgart, Nagoya, or Detroit—if not for GrabCAD.

Sasank learned of GrabCAD from Fateh Merrad, a GrabCAD member and friend he'd met through their shared passion for car design. "At the time I joined GrabCAD, I had just graduated from university and was applying for jobs as a product designer," he recalls. His timing could not have been better.

A month after Sasank joined us, Jerod Shelby, founder and chief designer of SSC North America (formerly Shelby SuperCars Inc.) issued a Challenge to the GrabCAD community. Impressed by the response to an earlier Challenge, this time Shelby upped the ante by challenging the community to come up with a comprehensive interior design concept for SSC's new supercar, the Tuatara.

"They were looking for a cutting-edge interior for the already complete exterior body design of their new supercar. It was a dream come true for me. I couldn't believe it," Sasank says. So he got straight to work and soon submitted a fully elaborated concept.

Jerod Shelby was thrilled with the result. To Sasank's enduring shock and delight, he was declared the Challenge winner. After reviewing Sasank's concept with SSC's engineering team, Shelby sent back a list of amends that Sasank incorporated into his final design.

"I finalized the car's interior design in about two weeks, and to this day, Jerod Shelby and I stay in touch," Sasank says. "We are both looking forward to the opportunity to move forward and realize the interior from a 3D to a physical one."

Shortly after winning the Tuatara Challenge, Sasank accepted a position as an industrial designer with India's BRG Group, a manufacturer of stainless steel products. "Since I started working late in 2011, I haven't had the time to visit GrabCAD as frequently as I would like," he says apologetically. "However, I have been an observer of its progress through some of the members' work."

Sasank will never forget his GrabCAD experience or the tremendous thrill of winning the Challenge. "It was a great morale booster for me," he says. "I proved to myself that I was capable of competing in international competitions. Through my participation in this Challenge, I've gained many contacts, including some very important and internationally known people. Without GrabCAD I would still be doing 3D models but would not have been

(*continued*)

(*continued*)

able to showcase my 3D skills to such great effect to an international audience."

Tommy Mueller and Verislav Mudrak

Tommy Mueller:

> Member since June 2012
>
> GrabCAD score: 13,698

Verislav Mudrak:

> Member since January 2012
>
> GrabCAD score: 66,893 (#1)

Growing up in Northern California in the 1980s, Tommy Mueller was a fan of sci-fi writers Isaac Asimov and Gene Roddenberry. He was intrigued by their ability to not only conceive imaginative and inspiring ideas but to put it all down on paper.

"In my view, this is what GrabCAD has done; it's given us the ability to put imagination down on paper. And now it's time to open the book." In other words, GrabCAD has made it easier to focus imagination into outputs that can inspire others and enable them to turn innovative concepts into physical objects.

For decades, Tommy worked with his hands more than his imagination, fabricating sailing masts for racing and cruising yachts. He would cut and drill the raw materials, grain and sand the edges, and weld the pieces together. Now living in Portland, Oregon, what excites him is the ability to use that craft knowledge in a virtual world. "Today, with 3D CAD, we can think and build accurately without entering the shop environment or using raw materials," he says.

Tommy's mother was on his case for years, urging him to work with his head instead of his hands. "She used to say to me, 'Think smarter and harder,'" he says with a grin. But it was his girlfriend who finally got him to do what Mom told him to, by giving him a SolidWorks Essentials course as a birthday present. He was immediately hooked.

"With CAD tools I realized that I could both model and make," he says. "At the time I was building store fixtures. I tried to get the company I was working with to move me into SolidWorks, but they were not willing to do so." So he quit.

The turning point came at the end of 2012, when a friend turned him on to GrabCAD. Soon after he joined, Tommy was inspired to invite the community to join his pet project: a life-sized cityscape in SolidWorks. This became one of the first open engineering projects on the site.

"Engineers from all over the world began to participate," Tommy recounts proudly. "They'd claim a building location to model, upload their model with renderings, and share it with other collaborators." Tommy assembled uploaded files into the cityscape, which he calls SolidWorks City. "For me, assembling these files from around the world gave me insight into the future: a newer,

(continued)

(*continued*)

more imaginative future that will bring us closer to our common goals. Open engineering will open doors to new possibilities, which will lead to innovation and ingenuity."

When the project was completed, he released it to the GrabCAD community, where members could download the project with a single click of a mouse. In fact, anyone can visit Tommy's city (I think we should call it Tommygrad) via the GrabCAD site.

A Meeting of Two Very Different Minds

Just like any of the world's great physical cities with a diverse populace, people from all over the world are meeting up in SolidWorks City and coming up with new ideas. To my mind, the most significant of these came when Tommy Mueller met Verislav Mudrak.

Supposedly, Verislav lives in Serbia, in a town near Belgrade. But I half suspect that he physically resides somewhere in our GrabCAD server. You can find him in the community almost 24/7, answering questions, uploading models, and commenting constructively about models others have posted. You can tell by his GrabCAD score, which is about to pass 67,000 as I write. That's more than 14,000 points ahead of our current number two, Renato Lunardini Jr. of Brazil.

Although they have yet to meet in person, Tommy calls Verislav "one of the most amazing designers out there." And he credits Verislav's help for turbocharging his own CAD skills that are now the driving force behind a thriving one-man 3D solid modeling business.

"I have achieved so much by learning from Verislav's inspiring and exquisite modeling work," Tommy says. "[It has] enriched my learning and moved it forward in ways I could not have imagined. His models, his video games . . . he can read a model like others read a book."

Verislav grew up in Serbia, "loving drawing, painting, mathematics, and physics." Today, he is an engineer with his own company that designs and manufactures injection tools, press tools, deep drawing tools, and tools used to cast patterns. While searching the Internet for a 3D model of a Rubik's Cube in January 2012, he found what he was looking for on GrabCAD. "To download the model, I had to create a profile. That is how it all began."

Asked about his Everest-high GrabCAD score, Verislav laughs. "Early on, when I first joined, I uploaded many models in a conscious effort to build my score. My goal was simply to appear on the first page of the engineer listing pages. But I never expected to be first," he adds modestly.

GrabCAD, in Verislav's view, provides an opportunity for talented designers in all phases of their careers to learn and help one another.

"GrabCAD holds the largest bank of 3D models on the Internet, which is very useful for any engineer," he says. "And for young engineers, the opportunity to participate in Challenges, to win prizes, and to gain recognition is very important."

Tommy Mueller's popularity on GrabCAD has been a boon to his 3D solid modeling business, and Verislav

(continued)

(*continued*)

is very much part of his plans. "Verislav represents the best in engineering," Tommy says. "His models speak for themselves. He should be a big contender, and all he needs to get there is the right exposure. He lives in Serbia, where it is tough to make ends meet. I want to help him, to bring him in on projects, to give him a hand.

"Designers from other parts of the world offer a different perspective, and GrabCAD enables collaboration with talent from anywhere in the world."

Verislav is very much on board. "I look forward to working with Tommy. My work on his private projects has been a real pleasure." And while holding the highest score on GrabCAD has been of great value, he says, "I would give all my points for a few mugs of beer with Tommy Mueller . . . should it become possible."

When that day comes, the beer is on me.

Women: The Doors Are Open, so C'mon In!

Men comprise the vast majority of our GrabCAD community. That's an educated guess because we don't actually track the gender of our members. But it is a reflection of the gender imbalance throughout the discipline of mechanical engineering—and it is surely a problem. Consistently great design takes all the diversity in perspective and insight you can throw at the process, so we need more women in the game.

Still, it wouldn't be fair to say our profession is somehow a last bastion of male domination, because there is no effort, conscious or otherwise, to exclude women. In our own case, Sara Sigel, our very competent community manager, goes out of her way to welcome women to GrabCAD.

From what I can see, the roots of gender imbalance extend way back into childhood. When we ask our engineers how they got here, again and again the men say things like: "Just to see how they worked, I used to take apart every toy they gave me . . . until I got LEGO. Ever since I've been making things."

Right now, I'm at this very point with my own daughters, Lana (age four) and Mona (age two). They will play along when I suggest we get out the Duplo (LEGO's younger sibling), but we always seem to end up making "princess houses" for their dolls, who remain at the center of their imagination. There is no denying which way the prevailing wind blows, and no one wants papa to be a LEGO Nazi, so I've been trying a different approach. We're currently designing a birdhouse, starting by drawing it on paper. Once that's done, we're going to create a 3D CAD model before fabricating it on a 3D printer. If all goes well, soon it should be hanging on the wall in their room.

As a result, are my daughters going to end up as "CADicts" like me? I'm not going to hold my breath, nor am I going to hold a grudge against Barbie.

What I hope, though, is that my daughters find as much joy and fulfillment in designing objects as three

(continued)

(continued)

women in our GrabCAD community who spoke to us about their own experience: Nediane Mesquita, a Brazilian CAD professional and mechanical engineering student; Jenny Tseitlin, an Israeli jewelry and product designer; and Krista Casal, a self-taught CAD designer who lives in Portland, Oregon.

Nediane Mesquita (http://grabcad.com/nediane .mesquita-1), a community member since December 2012, says GrabCAD gave her the confidence to pursue a degree in mechanical engineering. It's a sound career choice given that her hometown, Caxias do Sul in southern Brazil, is one of the country's leading engineering centers. What's more, Nediane already works as a CAD designer, modeling culinary equipment for Arke, one of Brazil's leading companies in the field.

Nediane heard about GrabCAD while teaching SolidWorks. "A student introduced me to a site he was very excited about," she says. "I was blown away by the quality of the work I found. I could hardly believe it existed."

Undaunted by the lack of women in mechanical engineering, Nediane's career path was set. "I fell in love with engineering while teaching SolidWorks . . . the ability to imagine something, design it, and see it become reality," she says. "And the remarkable work of designers and engineers from every corner of the world on GrabCAD was a second major inspiration. I knew this was what I wanted to do for the rest of my life."

Since embarking on her mechanical engineering studies, Nediane says she has enjoyed the feedback and camaraderie of the GrabCAD community. "I knew that sharing and learning from others would be of incalculable value, and as a former teacher, I realize that sharing what you know is the best way to learn even more. I am on GrabCAD daily, and I love to see that I have messages in my inbox. I correspond with engineers from other parts of the world, especially India, and feel very much part of the community when I see that others have downloaded the motors and electrical components I have posted. GrabCAD removes borders and barriers or all kinds. I am very much a part of a community without barriers or borders. I feel that I belong."

Jenny Tseitlin (https://grabcad.com/jenny--3), who holds a master's degree in industrial design, established her own design studio in her native Israel in 2011. With CAD modeling and photorealistic rendering at the center of her efforts, Jenny designs custom jewelry, furniture, and other products. She happened on GrabCAD while searching online for industrial design competitions, just in time to participate in the Challenge to design an interior for SSC's Tuatara supercar. "This was my first attempt at automotive design," she says. "I had been thinking of designing a car for a long time, but it remained kind of a dream until I discovered the GrabCAD Challenges."

Jenny's participation in the Challenges has garnered attention from both industrial design companies and the media, plus highly valued support from fellow community

(*continued*)

(*continued*)

members. "Constant positive feedback from other members gives me strength to continue on the tough and traditionally male paths like automotive design," she says.

The community's open environment keeps her engaged: "Open engineering is the future of CAD, and I stand strongly for the concept. I will continue to take part in design challenges and establish myself as a mature industrial designer."

As for her advice to other women in design and mechanical engineering: "Never leave well enough alone!"

Anyone who imagines that women are somehow peripheral in all this should meet Krista Casal (http://grabcad.com/krista.casal-1), who jumped into the community with both feet after joining in July 2012. She describes herself as "monumentally motivated and inspired by being part of the GrabCAD community."

Although self-taught and relatively new to CAD, Krista says her freelance Web development and design capabilities are already in demand up and down America's West Coast. "I'm an autodidact by nature," Krista says. "I caught the bug the first time I helped a client realize their idea by creating a prototype from a sketch. We sent the CAD file to a 3D printer, and next thing you know, I'm holding something real in my hand. It was a powerful experience."

She has been a key figure in the SolidWorks City initiative (brought to GrabCAD by her close collaborator Tommy Mueller) and an active participant in numerous

Challenges and group projects. As a result, Krista has become a much-loved member of the community.

As for being a woman in a male-dominated profession, Krista is unfazed: "For me, it's not a man's world at all. It's a world of possibilities." And she encourages other women to get in the game: "I like change and challenge, and we're at a very interesting place and exciting time. Today's software makes the paths to entry less rigid. You can learn CAD. It takes time and dedication, but you can learn."

For Krista, one of the best things about the community is how global and inclusive it is: "I am interested in how someone from another culture or part of the world imagines things, thinks about things and goes about things differently. Being part of such a vast and active community allows me to see and share in ways that would otherwise be impossible."

Executive Takeaways

- Research tells you only what's true today, not what will be true tomorrow. Everyone told us that sharing wouldn't work.

- Openness is a powerful force in a connected world. How can you break down the barriers in your business?

- What online communities do your customers and employees belong to, and how could you tap into those communities for new ideas and for talent?

- How are people in your industry reinventing the wheel? Are they focused on activities that don't bring value to your customers?

- What in your company is "too sacred to share"?

4 New Culture, New Tools Converge in the Cloud

For all the talk about The Cloud, so far you may have no earthly use for it. You don't need to run your word processor on someone else's server, and your hard disk likely has enough storage to hold all the family photos you will ever snap. But if you're an engineer, the cloud opens up a new universe.

Today's typical engineering workstation boasts compute power beyond the dreams of the team behind NASA's space missions of the 1960s and 1970s. As the *New York Times* recently noted, Voyager 1, launched in 1977, "carries an 8-track tape recorder and computers with one-240,000th the memory of a early iPhone."

And yet we can always use more. In fact, mechanical engineers will find creative ways to hog all the compute power you can throw at us. We need the cloud because it promises to provide a near-infinite amount of it.

Most of the stuff we do in three-dimensional computer-aided design (3D CAD) runs superbly with the resources that today's engineers have to work with. But there are definitely moments when some of us wish we could set a supercomputer loose on the task at hand—as with simulated testing, for example.

Will the exterior of my spacecraft survive the intense heat of reentry into the Earth's atmosphere? How will the exhaust gases flow in the combustion chamber of the rotary engine I'm working on? What will happen to the front end of my super-car design in a 30-mile-per-hour collision? Complex physical simulations such as this can require immense processing power—power that you may already have at your fingertips if you work at NASA or Nissan.

By delivering a quantum leap in processing power to any engineer with high-speed Internet and a credit card, the cloud threatens to disrupt the inherent advantages of scale and location. In other words, from here on it's no longer where you are or how big you are; it's the strength of your idea, your ability to rally others around it, and your skill and agility in execution. This is not to say that this means the end of big companies: Deep pockets and the ability to marshal vast resources still matter. But "big" has less of an inherent edge, and slow and stupid become bigger liabilities.

Physical simulation is only one facet of the potential for cloud-based engineering tools. By leveraging artificial intelligence and so-called big data, the tools of tomorrow may be able to test future designs against any real-world scenario ever recorded. For example, how would that car design have fared in every head-on collision cataloged since WWII? Or, how would the materials in that design degrade over time in the context of every climate on Earth?

If Japanese car designers had access to such a tool, they might have anticipated the effect that the salt spread on the roads in North America to melt ice would have. Instead, the corrosion problems that resulted because they didn't plan for this effect nearly sank Toyota in the early 1970s.

In a global economy, that kind of planetary wisdom is increasingly indispensable, but it's impossible for any individual engineer in Schenectady or Stuttgart to even aspire to. Who could even imagine that putting a hole of a certain size or shape in a design might mean that in Peru an anaconda could crawl into it?

By enabling engineers to apply more raw compute power to design problems, cloud computing makes it possible to analyze a much wider spectrum of risks. Thousands of alternative models can be run in parallel, making simulation a discovery tool instead of a mere validation tool. Here are some of the new simulation tools that the cloud will put within everyone's reach:

- *Structural optimization tools* will automatically analyze initial designs, tweaking their dimensions and reshaping their geometry to improve strength and minimize use of materials. In this way, rough concepts will be instantly transformed into optimal designs.

- *"Trade studies"* automatically analyze design solutions against their fundamental requirements, such as weight, cost, and capacity, to ensure the optimal approach has been followed. These tools will better inform business decisions.

- *Computational fluid dynamics*, a highly useful tool in many applications, allows a designer to examine how an object moves through water or air (both considered fluids by engineers). But as it is a notorious hog of processing power, access to it has been limited. From here on, cloud computing is going to make it much more widely available.

- *Multiphysics analysis* combines an astounding range of functionality—fluid dynamics, mechanics, electricity, chemistry, and other disciplines—into a single model. This type of analysis is like having your device interact with the real world, subject to all the forces of life.

- *Drop testing and crash testing* are crucial but hugely expensive to do physically. Even if you don't need the full rig that car-makers require (crash-test dummies and all), it's better to do this virtually before wasting all your prototypes. Of course, you can imagine the insane amount of compute power this requires. Only the cloud can bring this within reach. (Then again, you can send your prototype to Blendtec for testing in their brilliant "Will it blend?" marketing videos on YouTube. Watch what they do to an iPhone.)

What's more, the cloud will provide access to new tools that help product creators locate the best contract manufacturer for their needs, allowing them to source materials at lowest possible cost and work through the logistical economics of the supply chain.

Imagine this: As all this artificial intelligence and compute power come within their reach, individual engineers will have almost godlike creative power.

Still, there will never be a substitute for good old-fashioned human brainpower, especially when it's harnessed in cohesive teams. That's why the cloud's real and immediate relevance is its ability to make collaboration easier.

All Heads Converge in the Cloud

For me, this is where it gets really exciting. Coming from one side, we see the cloud putting powerful new tools within reach of start-ups and individual engineers. On the other side, in our GrabCAD community, we see, in front of our eyes, one million engineers and designers developing a new collaborative culture that empowers start-ups and individual creators.

A new culture and new tools are emerging at *exactly* the same moment. It's an awe-inspiring convergence, like looking up into the heavens and watching an eclipse. The electrifying challenge is to create the collaborative tools to support this convergence.

Remote collaboration isn't new, of course. Since the prehistoric 1,200-baud era, engineers have been exchanging CAD files by modem and FTP. More recently, they have been doing it via file-sharing services such as Dropbox.

But collaboration remains clunky. At worst, it's like the "cone of silence" on *Get Smart*, the 1960s spy comedy. When Max (the hapless spy hero who looks to me a lot like Vladimir Putin) needed to have a secret conversation with his boss, a plexiglas cone would descend from the ceiling to cover their heads. The gag was that once inside the cone, one couldn't hear a word the other one said.

In the real world it has been almost that bad. File versions get out of synch as bits and pieces of projects are scattered in hard drives throughout the team. Laptops get left in airport restrooms. E-mail attachments fall victim to hackers.

Even where collaboration is well organized, under the status quo the work remains locked inside CAD programs that are accessible only by the "priesthood," the engineers and designers who are equipped with the full and correct 3D CAD package. That makes it difficult to show other stakeholders—management, marketing, purchasing, or suppliers—how the project is progressing. They are completely locked out, so their feedback fails to make it into the loop.

It is a problem that is now widely recognized. And solving it is one of the best uses of the cloud that has been identified so far. It has also been a major frustration for our GrabCAD community. So using their input, we set out to design a collaborative tool geared to meet the needs of open engineering, as our community is defining it.

The key is to get the right balance between easy, accessible, and universal:

- *Easy* enough that anyone can see what's going on, even non-engineers who have never seen CAD in their lives.

- *Accessible* so that users can see their data and updates wherever they are. With the cloud, it's easy to make data accessible to any computer, but today, users expect to have access from smartphones and tablets as well.

- *Universal* in terms of being able to support all CAD platforms and any other kind of file a user might care to share on a project, such as photos, video, or text.

That was our goal in building a new kind of collaboration tool, Workbench, which we introduced in early 2013. It allows engineers, designers, marketers, suppliers, and anyone else to see a 3D model, stay up to date on changes, and contribute input.

Of course, we are not the only ones producing collaboration tools like this. For example, electrical engineers now have tools such as Upverter that allow them to share circuit designs, and for designers, there is a community called Behance. What's different about our approach is that we are focusing on mechanical engineers and the specific tools they use, 3D CAD in particular. And with roughly one-third of the world's 3D CAD users in our community, we're off to a strong start.

Our membership numbers are starting to draw the CAD software vendors to our party. Autodesk was the first to arrive via an agreement that puts their new pay-as-you-go CAD-in-the-cloud tools—AutoCAD 360 and Fusion 360—on our Workbench.

The June 2013 launch of this was great fun for me. Thirty months after this random Estonian had snuck into the Las Vegas press event to give an elevator pitch to Carl Bass, there I was, in Boston, cohosting a webcast with Carl, in San Francisco—CEO to CEO—to mark the occasion. Our demonstration was watched by thousands of engineers.

We staged the demonstration—which you can still find online (okay, maybe not if you're a historian reading this in 2050)—as if it was a real design meeting to discuss development of the handgrip and nozzle for a firefighter's hose. Acting as the supplier, I uploaded 3D CAD files to share with Carl, who played the client-side engineer. Since he could see the design immediately in Workbench, he was able to make changes on the spot, first pointing to the areas of concern and sketching out what he wanted, then making the changes directly. He decided that the hand grip was not sufficiently ergonomic, so he modified it right there and then. We focused on the work itself, without getting bogged down in a discussion of how we were going to exchange files.

The engineers watching the webcast around the world live were floored. Never before had anyone done anything like this. From opposite sides of the continent, we were able to collaborate as effortlessly as if we were in the same room. What's more, you don't even need a computer to do it. From now on, an engineer on the road will be able to keep tabs on a project and field client queries from a tablet. And if the customer demands an immediate change, the engineer can do it from an Internet café in China if necessary. It no longer matters where you are; collaboration is becoming seamless.

I am hoping to repeat the experience with the other three main CAD vendors. As I write this, we are talking with all of them, so I by the time you read this, I hope and expect everyone will be on board.

Wrapping Heads around a New Business Model

Still, some industry executives have trouble getting their heads around the idea of appearing on the same stage as their rivals. To get over this obstacle, I have to explain it in terms of real-world retail.

When deciding where to locate a brick-and-mortar store, you strive to position it where the customers go. But when you have the four biggest players in a particular category, one on each corner of an intersection, then that place becomes a magnet for whatever it is you sell. Or so I understand.

The CAD honchos had better get their heads around it, because the same tsunami of price destruction that leveled music and publishing is heading straight for the CAD vendors.

These vendors still have customers who are paying $10,000 per seat for CAD packages that they don't fully understand how to use and, in some cases, that they don't use every day. Plus, they are paying a 20 percent annual "maintenance fee" to get a software upgrade every two years. Adding insult to injury, the customers are locked in—which they absolutely hate.

Maybe customers could rationalize all this if they felt that every penny they spent was vital for research or if they received incredibly good support and training. But everyone knows that a big chunk of what they spend goes to support a distribution network of VARs—so-called value-added resellers—that don't actually add a lot of value. Many GrabCAD members tell us they were introduced to CAD through VAR training that did not teach them much and that their skills took off only once they joined the community and began taking our tutorials.

Even worse, the VARs isolate the CAD vendors from their customers. If you want to give feedback to Dassault Systèmes, believe it or not, at one point you've had to buy a customer feedback module. But the vendors don't feel any of it because the VARs take most of the heat.

Then there is the whole issue of upgrades. When a new software version comes out, it typically takes months to transfer old CAD models to the new package. Even then, the transfer is not guaranteed to work. The first releases are usually pretty buggy, so most customers will wait till the second or third one. You can't even test whether your data conversion will work without committing to an upgrade, so for all concerned it's a huge leap in the dark.

All of this is completely insane when you compare it to what you can do using tools in the cloud. With cloud-based software, you can see in real time how real people interact with your product, and you can improve it accordingly.

At GrabCAD, we have learned this lesson by building our Workbench tool in close collaboration with our user community. If any users encounter a problem with Workbench, they can click the icon on every page that says "I wish this page would . . ." And the chief executive officer (CEO) receives an immediate notification. I know because that's me. If you are having trouble uploading a new file version, you can click "request file support." That generates an e-mail to everyone in our company, creating a huge level of awareness that usually results in the bug being fixed within minutes. This approach strips bureaucracy out of product management and keeps our engineering customers happy. And as everyone knows (or should know), "happy engineers create better products."

Contrast this approach with having to buy a customer feedback module.

The Exciting Part

We are just getting to the really exciting part. A new collaborative culture is taking shape. New cloud-based tools are emerging. And we now have the platforms needed to facilitate collaboration. The stage is set.

What will the world's engineers and designers do on this new stage? Your guess may be as good as mine. In the following chapters I will share what I see coming up in various facets of the design and product development process.

Executive Takeaways

It's difficult to find a company today that does not use computers, and everyone has data that need to be shared. In your business:

- What's the most difficult type of information for your employees to share?

- What do your customers wish they knew about your business or product?

- What does a customer need to do to let the CEO know about a problem?

5 Design Challenge

Break Down the Monastery Doors

Sooner or later, every wave is bound to crash on the shore. And for the wave of change sweeping product design, that shore is the rock-hard immensity of mega-corporate process.

To say there is something grossly deficient in the closed and inflexible way that large companies design and develop products is hardly controversial. By now, I expect even remote tribes in the Upper Amazon have heard of the "not-invented-here syndrome." My favorite example is how Xerox invented the mouse but ignored it because the "wrong people" came up with the idea, only to have the young Steve Jobs come along and scoop it up to transform the personal computer industry. And even the dimmest smartphone buyer can tell you how Apple trumped Sony's silo mentality by combining every conceivable function in a single device that fits in the palm of the hand.

It's not hard to see why.

Corporate product development establishments are eerily like medieval monasteries. The lanyard-wearing monks sit in their cubicles, cloistered behind card-lock doors, adhering to a strict hierarchy and bound by a code of secrecy. Although they no longer illuminate scrolls, corporate monks work on three-dimensional computer-aided design (3D CAD) with the same solitary intensity. Many enter the order as youngsters and do not leave until retirement.

The analogy may be exaggerated, but not by much. I ran up against this attitude in my first job working for a door maker in Estonia. When it was suggested that we extend our product range and do a line of wooden doors, the answer from the old guys was: "We make metal doors, not wood." End of discussion.

On the positive side, monasteries can be deep reservoirs of craft skill handed down over generations—which is great if you're making beer or cheese. If you need a radically different and fresh approach, though, it is probably better to look beyond the people who developed the last 10 generations of whatever product you make.

Realizing how important it is for their monks to feel the wind outside the monastery walls, marketing and product development teams try hard to channel the breeze by packaging consumer research into formats the monks can grasp, such as buyer persona profiles. For example, automotive engineers get snapshots like this: "Julie, 27, is a condo sales rep from Pasadena who enjoys hot yoga and mountain biking on weekends. To her, performance means pert acceleration when the light turns green and she steps on the gas."

Working from such clues the monks strive to develop matrixes—"seats this soft; brakes this hard"—that capture what Julie wants. But it's already like designing for Martians—and it's only going to get tougher. In the global marketplace, targets are becoming ever more diverse and elusive, and the product cycle gets shorter and shorter each year.

While Japanese engineers have always had to work hard to get inside the heads of Western consumers, Americans have had it relatively easy until now. Those able to produce a hit with Los Angeles buyers have been able to count on success in the huge U.S. market, plus a global appetite for California cool.

In this new environment, the winners will be those who can draw and shoot quickly and precisely at multiple targets that may be well over the horizon: China's "Little Emperors" as they move into middle age, the changing dynamics of multi-generational Indian families, the upwardly mobile aspirations of empty-nesters in Brazil . . . and don't forget my mother-in-law in Estonia.

Here's a prediction: As the global center of gravity shifts away from mature markets, the emerging-market middle classes are not going to accept hand-me-down solutions from here on. They are going to want designs informed by their specific functional needs.

Where are major corporations going to get that kind of eclectic and panoramic perspective? There is no way around it. The monastery doors must swing open to admit a wider spectrum of input: from colleagues and customers—and from external design and engineering talent.

To those who have spent their entire careers behind the walls, all this is deeply scary. And the scariest prospect of all is the risk that outsiders will have access to the holiest of holy, the sacred intellectual property. If that's your concern, stop worrying and look at who is going for open engineering and how they are doing it.

Who's Taking the GrabCAD Challenge?

There can be few people on the planet who better understand the importance of protecting the value of intellectual property than Paolo Termini. Over the course of 20 years, Paolo's company, 500 Group, bought the patent rights to thousands of mechanical devices and functions. Then it made sure that companies using techniques covered by its patents paid a reasonable licensing fee for the privilege. There is a rude name for unscrupulous operators in the same business, but it does not apply to Paolo—so don't even think of it.

Six years ago, however, Paolo sold all his patents and poured the proceeds into an ambitious venture aimed at reinventing the way supercars are designed, built, and sold (see the feature that follows). As a patent guy, you might expect his new business model to be based on keeping everything under wraps. Instead, the complete opposite is true; Paolo has become one of open engineering's biggest fans—and he's jumped in with both feet.

500 Group: Yo, Ferrari, Check Your Rearview

The same goes for Lamborghini and every other supercar maker, because a million engineers are now on their tails. Meet the man to blame. . . .

Paolo Tiramani, the chief executive officer (CEO) of 500 Group, is no stranger to invention. An industrial designer and mechanical engineer, Tiramani started the Greenwich, Connecticut-based firm as an intellectual property (IP) licensing company in 1986. Over 20 years, it collected hundreds of millions of dollars in patent licensing fees for basic mechanical goods and automotive and mechanical devices. Six years ago, the company made a bold change in direction. "We sold the majority of patents to Stanley Black & Decker," says Paolo. "Since that time I have focused on two areas: habitat manufacturing and automotive."

Paolo began looking at price and value in the high-performance automotive niche. "High-performance cars come with stratospheric price tags, with supercar prices hovering in the $300,000 to $400,000 range. I looked at these numbers as an inventor and a designer and saw an opportunity to create a lower-cost entry for this market."

"We set out to work in an alternative way," says Paolo, "and to deliver stratospheric performance at a 75 to 80 percent reduction in cost." The company secured a special-projects supply agreement with GM to provide performance parts hardware and the GM V8 line of E-Rod LS3, LS7, and mighty 638-hp supercharged LS9 engines. "We began a unique crate engine business."

Open Sesame

Paolo's alternative approach has been to embrace open source engineering, which is not what you might expect from a guy who made his living from securing intellectual property. But as he explains it, "Both the open source and protectionist models have merit. Focusing on the end result helps to clarify the question of which might be better. Lest we forget the purpose of business is to make money by providing value. Open source is not altruism; it's simply a different path to that result."

He continues, "Typically open source works best when the founding company controls the 'boat' and invites 'barnacles' to attach to it, and there are lots of examples. The Apple ecosystem with its apps is one form; what we

(continued)

(continued)

are doing with our own automotive IP, by enabling others to create their own bodies, is another. The principle is the same, whereby the founding company has the ability to generally steer the enterprise and to profit somewhere in the food chain—even if it's not a direct profit from the point of sale. Open source can sound very Zen-like, but at the end of the day, the destination is the same."

What we appreciate is that Paolo chose GrabCAD's open source engineering platform as the preferred route to his destination by way of posing a Challenge to the community.

"In 2012, we needed to explore and develop a number of body styles for our performance car system," he says. "The skill and feel are in the chassis, while the car's body pushes air and looks gorgeous. But the car's body is the emotional element, and it has massive play value. We were looking for a broad view. I cannot recall how GrabCAD came onto our radar, but I was interested in how to make use of this unique and passionate community."

The Supercar Body Challenge

500 Group posted its chassis and a brief along with a Challenge inviting the community to design two versions of their supercar body, a street body and a street-legal track body. Prizes included $3,500, the possibility of additional work, and invitations to test tracks in Europe, Africa, and the United States.

From an extraordinarily high volume of quality entries, a jury then chose three designs in each category and submitted them to a vote by the community.

"The results wildly exceeded our expectations," Paolo says, "with over 200 entrants and body style submissions. There was simply no other resource available anywhere that could harness that kind of professional power in terms of speed, volume, and diversity of ideas and talent."

Pleased with the outcome, 500 Group created a GrabCAD Superteam, a select group of talented Challenge entrants to continue the collaboration. "This is an industry first," Paolo says.

. . . and Just-in-Time Delivery from GrabCAD

The conclusion of 500 Group's first Challenge coincided with the launch of GrabCAD's Workbench. "The folks at GrabCAD must have been reading our minds," says Paolo. "Exactly when we needed it, they provided a collaboration tool for our newly created team . . . a great venue to share ideas and communicate—often in incredible detail. Never before have I been able to manage a design team not in the same room. I'm collaborating in a serious venture with designers from all over the world."

The quest continued as 500 Group challenged the community to create an instrument panel as simple and purely functional as possible, with a layered sense of depth, floating three-dimensional elements, and extensive use of color and animation to convey functional

(continued)

(continued)

information to the driver. Again, the GrabCAD community passed with flying colors.

Now 500 Group is planning a second GrabCAD body design contest—this time on their production chassis—"with a view to holding a worldwide public referendum of the winning entrants in the mainstream press," says Paolo. "Effectively, it's a worldwide focus group to ensure we bring the most beautiful, popular product to market . . . another industry first powered by GrabCAD."

The company is looking forward to engaging the world in its supercar body design. "We need the feedback," says Paolo. "We can measure engineering, but not the body, the least functional but most emotional aspect of our car."

Paolo encourages others to "go fishing in GrabCAD's million-strong community. It's as deep a pool of talent as we have. Use their collaboration tool and design challenges. There is nothing like it. GrabCAD put us on an equal footing with Ford and GM."

Personally, I can't wait for the chance to drive one of Paolo's supercars. I just hope he can bring it in at a price point that my wife will sign off on!

There are lots of ways to explore the potential of an open approach. To dip one toe in, you can explore the models on our site and reach out to engineers whose work intrigues you. Conversely, you can dive in with a big splash and pose a GrabCAD "Challenge" to our community (as outlined in Chapter 3).

No surprise that supercar makers don't go for the slow, gradual approach. Guys like Jerod Shelby of SSC and Paolo Termini of 500 Group don't waste time when the light turns green. So just as Shelby challenged the community to do a comprehensive interior concept for his Tuatara (and found our man Sasank Gopinathan), Termini's challenge was to do two complete exterior body designs for his new supercar.

It's no surprise that engineers in our community dived on the challenge. Even the daydream of designing the exterior of a supercar is enough to make us gearheads hyperventilate. So before you could say "supercar," 200 of our engineers had put hundreds of hours into submissions that blew Paolo's socks off.

As a result, 500 Group invited the top Challenge contenders to join a special project team that is working with the company on an ongoing basis via Workbench, GrabCAD's proprietary collaborative tool. That process led to another Challenge to the community, this time for an IP. No, not intellectual property; in the car biz an IP is an instrument panel. And plans are afoot for a chassis Challenge.

From our viewpoint, all this is fantastic. Skeptics, however, have told me it's much what they would expect: experimentation by new players who aspire to disrupt the established order. The heavy hitters, they say, are never going to embrace "this open thing."

Oh, yeah? Tell that to GE.

General Openness

In electrical and mechanical engineering, enterprises don't come bigger or broader than GE. From jet engines and locomotives to power generation and medical devices down to home appliances,

GE is a giant with an enormous reach. And it is an unusually smart giant. "Imagination at work" is GE's brand statement . . . and from what I've seen, GE means it.

Since launching GrabCAD, we've had flickers of interest from a number of large companies, as well as some serious attention from a few such as Nokia. But ever since GE began to explore what they call "Open Innovation," we have really felt the warmth of its attention. So have many other start-ups in our space, such as Quirky. GE is the most sophisticated buyer of engineering in the business—and their management realizes something important is happening.

In June 2013, GE put some skin in our game: a Challenge to test the water (see the following feature). GE asked our community for suggestions on how to make an innocuous little part, a bracket that is used to lift a jet engine for maintenance, lighter and stronger. They thought maybe they would get 100 submissions that would save perhaps 20 percent in weight. I think we kind of blew their minds.

GE's Amazing Weight Loss Challenge

For the world's largest engineering concerns, open engineering is unexplored territory, a modern-day equivalent to the Upper Amazon. Most have only a dim idea what to expect if they venture up-river. But one of mega-engineering's most intrepid explorers was amazed by the potential they discovered.

GE, one of the world's largest and most innovative engineering conglomerates, wisely keeps a close eye on the evolution of design and engineering at the start-up level. So having watched from on high the exponential growth of the GrabCAD community, the Connecticut-based giant decided to try an experiment.

On June 12, 2013, GE posted a Challenge to the GrabCAD community, calling for new designs for a small bracket used to hold jet engines in place. As it was nothing glamorous like designing a supercar, they—and we at GrabCAD—had no idea whether the community would even be interested, especially in the dog days of summer.

"This Challenge was the first of its kind for us with GrabCAD," says GE's Alex Tepper. "With additive manufacturing removing some of the constraints of traditional manufacturing, we proposed the challenge of redesigning a simple bracket that had remained relatively unchanged for decades. We were looking for improvements to size and weight and to test the waters of GrabCAD's open-innovation platform."

Small though the part is, redesigning it was not a simple task. "It was, in fact, a highly technically challenging one," Alex says. "It involved simulation criteria, 3D printing capabilities, additive manufacturing knowledge, high-end software—all aspects that we felt would seriously narrow the field of entrants."

So expectations were low, and as GE's global director of innovation, Alex's main goal was to explore the potential

(continued)

(*continued*)

of open engineering. "I am always asking and looking at what we can learn from the outer world. We know that recent advances in 3D printing are supposed to have far-reaching implications for design and manufacturing. As much as open engineering challenges the established culture at GE, I wanted to explore how it could be disruptive, how we could speed our time to market and improve our products, and add open innovation to our global brand."

While GE prides itself on employing the best and brightest, Alex acknowledges that the company employs only a sliver of the remarkable engineering and design talent out there. "The outside world has a lot to offer—outside engineering and scientific minds bring a wider perspective to the table," he says. "It represents opportunities for cross-pollination of ideas and access to a good and talented cross-section of great minds from every corner of the world."

After the deadline for submissions on August 9, Alex and his colleagues were astonished at how far beyond their expectations the community had gone.

"We received 697 entries from 56 countries," he says, "but we would have been thrilled with 100 submissions." They were even more astounded when it came time to judge the entries. "We anticipated a weight reduction of around 20 percent. The top 10 entries delivered between 75 and 85 percent reductions in weight."

In a large aircraft with multiple brackets, these numbers could represent a weight reduction of several hundred pounds. "The implications are astonishing," Alex says. "If we could apply this learning to numerous other simple parts, we could lower the overall weight of the engine by 20 percent."

Ten finalists, chosen by a panel of judges, advanced to phase 2 of the Challenge. "Besides the top 10 finalists, we were compelled to add a category of honorable mentions to acknowledge the range of breathtaking approaches and gorgeous designs of seven additional submissions," Alex said.

In phase 2, in process at time of writing, the top 10 entries will be 3D printed in metal and tested to ensure they live up to stress and strength criteria. "We are also producing video profiles for each finalist. We will be filming them at their workstations, interviewing them, getting to know who they are, and learning where they live and work," Alex said. GE will share the finalists' profiles on GrabCAD, YouTube, and other social media outlets.

For Alex, this Challenge represents a turning point for traditional companies. "Intellectual property (IP) has traditionally been sacrosanct. While IP will always be important, it would seem that more high-end minds at work in an open innovation setting trumps IP," he said.

GE's board of directors, when presented with the Challenge results, immediately recognized its value and directed Alex and his team to draft a plan for moving forward with open innovation. "They embraced it whole-heartedly and quickly. This is an exciting time for GE . . .

(continued)

(*continued*)

a huge cultural shift. We need to incubate this and move
forward properly. These changes will be transformative for
business," he said.

Having now seen what's up the unexplored river, Alex is
convinced that with the convergence of digitization, democ-
ratization, and decentralization, mid- and large-sized companies alike stand to be disrupted, and soon: "What used to
cost start-ups $5 million in 1998, today costs $50,000 dollars, and the evolution continues, exponentially faster. The
writing is on the wall. Evolve quickly. Evolve or you will be
disrupted by someone you don't even see coming."

For the GrabCAD community, to be "discovered" so
enthusiastically by a company that mechanical engineers
admire, perhaps more than any other, has been a huge
validation. I would say we are no longer way up the river;
we are now the new mainstream.

In phase 1 of the Challenge, their team received 697 submissions from 56 countries, most of them from engineers outside
the aerospace industry. That alone would have impressed them.
Where we got to the mind-blowing stage was when they realized
that not one but more than a dozen of the submissions achieved
weight savings of 75 to 85 percent. Even better, they realized that by applying this learning to every component in the
engine they could reduce its overall weight by up to 20 percent.
Consider this against what one GE employee told me: that they
regularly spend billions of dollars to achieve single-digit reductions in engine weight.

So a weight savings of 20 percent really represents a quantum leap. In fact, weight is such an overriding concern that people at the airlines sit around thinking about ways to get the change out of your pocket before you board. Maybe that's how they came up with all their innovative ways to nickel-and-dime us.

Our GE friends were so excited they took the news all the way up the very steep ladder to GE's board of directors. And the board said, "Move forward with open innovation." To that, I say, "Praise the board, and pass the innovation!"

In fact, GE got so excited that shortly after the results came out, when Thomas Friedman, the famed columnist of the *New York Times*, toured GE's research center, they boasted about it to him. And that prompted Friedman to write a September 14, 2013, column "When Complexity Is Free" (www.nytimes .com/2013/09/15/opinion/sunday/friedman-when-complexity- is-free.html?_r=0) that said:

Example: There are parts of an aircraft engine—hangers, brackets, etc.—that are not key to the engine, but they keep it attached and add weight, which means higher fuel costs. So GE recently took one bracket—described the conditions under which it worked and the particular function it performed—and posted it online under the "The GE Engine Bracket Challenge." The company offered a reward to anyone in the world who could design that component with less weight, using 3-D printing.

"We advertised it in June," said Iorio. Within weeks, "we got 697 entries from all over the world" from "companies, individuals, graduate students and designers." G.E.'s engineers culled out the top 10, and they are now being tested to determine which is the lightest that conforms to G.E.'s specs and can be built on its printers. I saw one prototype that was 80 percent lighter than the older version. The winning prize pool is $20,000, spread out across 8

finalists, with awards ranging from $1,000 to $7,000 each.
A majority of entries came from people outside the aviation
industry.

The only problem with Friedman's account is that GE did not issue the Challenge to "anyone in the world"; it was to anyone in the GrabCAD community. But, hey, we are happy to get the word out about the power of open, so let's not quibble.

The bottom line is that the leader of the pack has spoken. GE has validated open engineering, and that means it is no longer the preserve of disruptive upstarts. So not only are young Turks in the monasteries now free to advocate change, all mega-corporate design establishments risk getting left behind if they don't get on board because, as Alex Tepper, GE's global director of innovation, points out:

What used to cost start-ups five million dollars in 1998, today
costs fifty-thousand dollars, and the evolution continues, exponen-
tially faster. The writing is on the wall. Evolve quickly. Evolve or
you will be disrupted by someone you don't even see coming.

The key benefit for GE is bringing more participants into the process—engineers from all over the world and from outside the aerospace industry who could not possibly afford the sophisticated tools that GE has. When you make it dramatically easier to play, you get a new set of players.

If all this prompts you to ask, "What am I being asked to sign on to?" it's a fair question and one I'll try to answer as best I can. But I hate making predictions, and I never want to set myself up as some futurist guru telling the world how it's going to be. So all I can tell you is what I see.

Sketching out a New Model for Design: Key Word Is "Collaboration"

What's the new model for industrial design? The honest truth is that, as yet, there is no paint-by-number pattern to follow. Instead, we can see hundreds of experiments in progress as companies and individual engineers explore a new frontier. All that said, we can also see several broad themes emerging.

Collaboration is the key word, because more of it is what is required to achieve greater accuracy in targeting, faster speed from concept to market, and lower cost.

Back to the monastery metaphor for just a moment. The problem with 3D CAD so far is that its immense wealth of knowledge and creative power has been available to only 3.1 million professionals around the world. Unless you have the right CAD software installed on your computer, you can't access CAD files. This creates the same situation we had when book learning was confined to the monasteries, that is, until Gutenberg introduced movable type to Western civilization (the Chinese and Koreans were already there).

Add to that a second related obstacle: In large engineering firms, CAD files already reside on huge product lifecycle management (PLM) systems that allow hundreds of engineers to work simultaneously on the same new car or aircraft. But in smaller-scale enterprises, until now, CAD files have been stored on individual hard drives or in-office networks; this has been a huge limitation on the scope for wide-scale collaboration.

That's why the biggest driver of change in design—this is not a prediction, it's already happening—is the destruction of the wall that has kept creativity locked inside our modern monasteries. Cloud computing is what makes it possible. New tools such as our own GrabCAD Workbench are what makes it practical.

What changes and benefits will cloud collaboration bring to the process?

- *All can see.* Whereas designs in process have been accessible only to CAD professionals, the new tools allow all trusted stakeholders—management, marketing, manufacturing, and business units on the other side of the world—to see progress in real time and provide input as necessary. In today's closed systems, by some estimates, for every content creator, there are 10 others who need to be informed about what is being created. What's more likely is that for every CAD creator, there are actually hundreds of people who need to see what's going on. Many of them are customers who want to be in the loop and who would love to give their input. When you can get that input early, and in rich detail, you get to market faster and much more accurately. All that remains to be developed is process discipline that affords more access to more cooks without spoiling the broth.

- *All can work simultaneously.* When all stakeholders have access to a common data model, the design process moves from sequential to simultaneous development. While engineers work on functionality under the skin, designers can perfect the look and feel, marketing can test the color scheme, purchasing can evaluate the material cost, suppliers can develop components, and manufacturing can work out how and where to put the product together. This is already how cars are made today; the change is that the same methodology is becoming universal.

- *New perspectives come into the picture.* As GE's Challenge
to our community demonstrates, any design establishment
can benefit from access to a wider pool of talent, even a
sophisticated engineering conglomerate that has the world's
top talent in-house. That value may come from specialized knowledge of materials or processes; it may come from
insight into the needs of distant markets. Or it may even
come simply from having a fresh perspective. The point is
that the talent pool outside the company is both broader and
deeper than the pool inside the company. When that talent
is organized as a community and you have the tools to make
collaboration viable, you can make sure you have the right
person on the job, wherever that person happens to be.

- *Flexible power when you need it.* Adding resources takes forever
today. Increased head count must be requested and approved.
A spec must be drawn up for human resources, which must
then scour the local talent pool or seek engineers willing to
move. Candidates must be interviewed . . . and on and on
and on. By contrast, the GE people put out a spec for the
actual work just before the summer holidays and came back
to find almost 700 submissions that exceeded their expectations. Crowdswarming will become the new norm. What
is true in terms of people also applies to the tools they use.
Today you can "rent" software for a crowd of summer interns
then turn off the applications when they go back to school in
the fall. With both people and technology, resources will be
increasingly available on an as-needed basis.

- *Efforts will be integrated.* Until now, design, marketing, and
manufacturing have been to a great extent autonomous
functions. Cloud-based collaboration will integrate them.
The factory (in China or wherever) will be in continuous

contact with design and engineering (in the United States or elsewhere). Likewise, marketers will be able to see the product before expensive prototypes are created. And as a result of better integration . . .

- *Quality is going to soar.* When the left hand doesn't know what the right hand is doing, quality inevitably suffers. Especially with complex devices involving hundreds of parts that are all constantly evolving, version control in the current system is extremely tricky. Once everyone is working from the same CAD model in the cloud, many quality issues are going to disappear.

- *Process will speed up.* With simultaneous, integrated development and flexible crowdswarming, the entire process from concept to store shelf is going to become a lot faster—and it's not going to stop. As soon as the launch version goes into production, design efforts will shift to creating variants, upgrades, and the next generation. Instead of a stop-and-go design process with monthly design reviews, engineers will receive constant input—no more waiting for the manager to return from a business trip to sign off on changes. The engineer will post an update to the cloud, and the manager will approve it using a mobile phone while waiting in an airport somewhere. Complex simulations will run in parallel in the cloud, returning results in minutes instead of grinding away all night on a desktop. The process will get faster at every step.

- *Costs are going to dive.* Material cost is a decisive factor in manufacturing. But in design, cost equals time. So a faster process inevitably means lower cost—and so does lower in-house head count. The ability to collaborate effectively with engineering talent anywhere on the planet creates huge leeway for low-cost sourcing. That doesn't necessarily imply a race to the bottom or offshore. When searching for a brain surgeon, which would you choose: the cheapest or the best? The same goes for mechanical engineers, people who actually *do* rocket science.

- *Competitors will be coming out of the woodwork.* Back to Alex Tepper's observation that what used to cost $5 million in product development now costs $50,000. The same goes for labor. What used to take 20 engineers working side by side full-time for a year can now be achieved by a small team collaborating remotely over a summer—or even by one individual. You no longer need a fortune or an army to go into developing physical products. And that means incumbents will see competitors coming from all over the place.

These are just some of the factors that will drive the evolution of the design process. Who will have the advantage in this process?

The winners will be those organizations best able to leverage the new culture and the new tools. And in this, the edge likely goes to start-ups, just because it is much easier to build a new corporate design culture from scratch than it is to change the entrenched ways of a large incumbent.

I also see the edge going to those who are open to what initially sound like crazy ideas. That is because anything that doesn't disrupt our fixed modes of thinking is probably not truly brilliant or original. Perhaps the best example of how to do this is Quirky, a cunningly crafted funnel that processes 2,000 ideas a week, sifting out the truly brilliant from the completely wacky (see the feature that follows). Significantly, GE is exploring ways to collaborate with Quirky as well. In a first initiative, GE has opened its vast database of in-house device patents to the Quirky community in hopes that fertile imaginations will spot overlooked opportunities for innovation.

Quirky Transforms "Not-Invented-Here" from Problem to Opportunity

The not-invented-here syndrome has been recognized as a huge obstacle to innovation for decades, but it was only five years ago that Quirky figured out how to turn an obstacle into an opportunity.

Quirky is an inventor's dream come true: a one-stop-shop with the expertise and technology needed to help anyone with a great idea bring innovative consumer product concepts to reality and to market. Since its inception, this New York–based start-up has developed nearly 400 consumer products, many sold by major retailers, including Walmart, Lowes, Target, Bed Bath & Beyond, and Home Depot, to name a few.

Founder Ben Kaufman learned how to overcome the obstacles from the ground up, having conceived of his first device, the Mophie, while still in high school. Named after his dogs, it was a headphone device on a cord, designed to be worn around the neck, that allowed him to listen to his iPod in math class, undetected.

That device became the foundation of an Apple accessories company of the same name that spawned, among other offerings, the Mophie battery pack. Ben sold Mophie in 2007 and founded Quirky at the age of 23 in 2009. Since then, he has raised more than $90 million in venture funding, and Quirky was ranked at 59 in the 2013 Forbes list of America's most promising companies.

"Quirky is a unique model," explains the company's senior design engineer, Nicholas Oxley. "Creating products and bringing them to market is difficult. There are many barriers to entry. Quirky takes down the barriers and acknowledges that anyone, from novice inventors to experts, can have a great idea. Everyone, whether they are aware of it or not, is affected by industrial design. And everyone, right down to the consumer, interacts with design and has insights into how well or badly design is working for them."

Every day, people from around the world—who must become members of the Quirky community—submit their product ideas to Quirky.com. "We receive anywhere from 1,500 to 2,000 new product ideas a week, in every format from back-of-the-napkin sketches to videos and CAD models with rendering," says Nicholas. "While we appreciate a physical prototype, no idea is rejected based on its level of detail."

Quirky renders and storyboards select ideas and posts them on its website. Then Quirky invites the 480,000 members of its online community to weigh in.

(continued)

(continued)

Products that make it through this vetting stage are presented for consideration at the company's live-streamed weekly EVAL meetings. "Community members vote for the most popular products. From here, a small number of products are chosen to go into production," Nicholas explains.

Quirky launches two products in the average week and shares revenues with inventors as well as community influencers and members of the community who have contributed to the development of successful products.

Products slated for manufacturing go through a more extensive prototyping phase at Quirky's advanced product facility in Manhattan, where in-house designers and engineers get down to the business of turning ideas into products. "We model to CAD, send to our 3D printers, and have parts within hours," says Nicholas. "It's a one-day turnaround to prototype once we have the CAD files."

Engineering and design teams very quickly iterate, making design changes and sending revisions to the 3D printers. "We have the highest-resolution 3D printers in the country. They allow us to use our engineers, our most creative and productive resource, effectively. Our creative talent is not off building models."

The team uses state-of-the-art prototyping equipment to produce objects as close as possible to the real thing, with structural parts printed in the same materials used in mass production. "We can do a drop test—we can abuse the parts if we want to. We create high resolution, repeatable, functionally sophisticated prototypes," Nicholas says.

This level of prototyping optimizes both products and time lines. "The more realistic the prototype, the better the engineering and the more dynamic and meaningful the iterative steps toward manufacturing," Nicholas says. "This predictability not only plays into the path to manufacturing; it gives us confidence in our end result."

Quirky's time-to-market record—from concept to shipped product—is 30 days. "It was a simple but unique product," Nicholas says. "This turnaround is remarkable. I have seen product development take two years in the course of my career."

Quirky's goal is to launch 24 products per quarter. "It's an aggressive schedule, and we don't always meet it," Nicholas admits, "but it's the goal."

Looking to the future, Oxley predicts that open innovation, enabled by new technologies, will empower designers to be more open than ever to diverse human experiences and observations and allow the public to become part of the iterative experience. "This ease of collaboration and iteration, this speed . . . as a designer it is a very satisfying and rewarding time. And it will even become more so and continue to impact manufacturing at every level," he says.

You need to reach deep into the realm of imagination because, as Steve Jobs so insightfully observed, "People don't know what they want until you show it to them."

On the execution side, as noted, integration is going to be critical. And in this, the fashion industry shows what the future may look like in other fields.

Zara, the retail chain owned by Spain's Inditex, takes just four or five weeks to go from initial design to the store rack. That compares with an industry average of six months. It's a miracle of very tight vertical integration and a finely tuned just-in-time process. Most stores and factories are company owned. Management, design, and key manufacturing plants are all clustered in northwest Spain. Because the design team is continually informed as to what's happening on the retail front line, if a certain product fails to move, Zara is able to swap it out pronto. Meanwhile, competitors with supply chains that stretch all the way to Bangladesh can do no more than say, "Oops, I guess we'll have to try harder next year."

The drivers will be different in each industry, but the paths all lead in the same direction: fresh ideas and laser-precise, lightning-fast reaction to shifts in market demand. Since the design process is the critical link in terms of imagination, precision, and speed, that's where change needs to start.

But where does the path begin? I believe the answers are different for big and small companies.

If Big, Start by Opening Inward

In a big company, if you start by advocating change that's too radical—say, parceling all the work out to engineers in the online community—you might find yourself getting frog-marched to the parking lot with the contents of your desk in a cardboard box. You may want to take a more incremental approach.

Start by building consensus around the fundamental principle that it is wise to bring more perspectives into the design process earlier—but in a disciplined way. The first line of resistance you are likely to hit will be, "Oh no, not more process; not more meetings; not more cooks with their hands in the soup." It is a fear that's not unfounded, because design teams everywhere have scars to show from drive-by design decisions made on a whim by senior management.

The way to get around that is to start with an exercise using the new cloud-based collaborative tools accessible to non-technical stakeholders—without requiring everyone to gather for a meeting.

Make the initial exercise internal, because the second line of resistance to a more open process is invariably about data security. Invite a diverse range of stakeholders: sales and marketing (especially key overseas markets), management, purchasing, and whomever else you like.

Give them a chance to look over the design team's shoulder and invite their feedback. But do it in such a way that the designers don't feel threatened by the experience. At the end of the exercise, ask everyone how they felt about it, summarize the feedback, and cascade it back to the participants. In the process, explain the benefits you hope to achieve with a more open approach.

As you build confidence, gradually widen the circle to include external but close stakeholders: suppliers, distributors, your advertising agency, consultants, and others.

Leverage the support of this wider group as you move toward the ultimate goal: bringing the voice of the customer into the design process as early and clearly as possible. Beyond focus groups and other standard market research tools, explore new ways to engage potential customers.

How can you leverage social media? How can you harness the near-magical 3D rendering power of CAD to showcase your designs in a virtual environment? This is where the action is on the frontier of design communication.

Once everyone is comfortable with having customers involved in the design process, it won't be a big leap to start bringing outside engineers and designers into the mix, especially young talent and perspectives from distant markets. For a fresh perspective, it's good to reach beyond the skill set assembled by your company's human resources department.

Start-Ups: You and Whose Army?

"You and whose army?" In the schoolyard, that's what bigger guys used to say to smaller guys who dared to stand in their way. But in design and product development, the small guy can now answer: "I'll be right back with my own army."

If your idea is compelling, if you are lucid and can earn the trust of your peers, and if you have sufficient resources behind you, today, on short notice, it is entirely possible to rally to your flag if not an army of engineers at least a small unit of elite commandos.

With more than one million CAD professionals now networked in an online community, an almost infinite reservoir of expertise is within reach. With track records and areas of specialization displayed transparently, you can easily recruit the specific skills needed to turn concepts into workable designs.

No need to start from scratch either. Today you can quickly deploy and modify open source components or scan and reverse-engineer physical parts. If you hit an obstacle, you can call on the community for advice on overcoming it. Even better, as outlined in Chapter 4, new cloud-based tools are emerging to help at every turn from material cost analysis through life cycle wear to manufacturing viability.

It is hard to overstate what all this does in terms of changing the game and opening doors for entrepreneurs who want to turn inspired ideas into viable products. Small teams can now move mountains—and can do so fast.

It May Look Good on Paper . . .

The CAD tools we have now can work wonders, generating renderings so realistic they seem almost real. But it has to be admitted: No matter how good our designs look on paper or in 3D on the screen, ultimately there is still no substitute for the real thing. Fortunately, it's getting easier to produce a physical prototype.

Executive Takeaways

Two things often prevent organizations from making big leaps forward. The first is a mistaken view of what "we do" and what "we don't do." Second is that companies draw lines around who gets to be "creative" and who is supposed to "just get things done." In a connected world, both of these sets of assumptions need to be taken out and shaken up a bit.

- What do you do that could benefit from crowdsourcing? How would you identify the right crowd to source from?

- What do you currently not do that would boost your business if you could tap the right people to do it (including people who may already work for you)?

- Are there opportunities to crowdsource ideas within your company, using people who are regarded as "not creative" to generate ideas?

- If you radically opened up one part of your business, what benefits would you see? What would the risks be, and how could you mitigate them?

6 Here's My Prototype; Please Kick the Crap Out of It

Surrounded by supermodel lookalikes, supercar prototypes sit like religious icons on the altars of sprawling motor shows from Frankfurt to Shanghai. You can look in awe at these concept cars, as the auto industry calls design prototypes, but don't dare lay a finger on one.

So what's the point? If no one can touch, much less sit in it or drive it, why spend up to $1 million on a piece of sculpture?

That's the problem with prototypes. They have always been rare and expensive—to the point that they fail to fulfill their intended function. As a consequence, year after year, new products go on the market with insufficient real-world testing. What manufacturers really need are prototypes they can hand out like free samples at Costco to those who fit the target buyer persona. Give it to the customer and say, "Here's my prototype; please kick the crap out of it."

Fortunately, virtually and physically, it's getting easier to do that right from the concept stage.

Virtual Is Virtuous . . .

Not so very long ago, there was not a lot you could show to a customer at the concept stage—maybe a two-dimensional artist's rendering or a clay model with a coat of paint. Only an engineer could imagine anything by looking at blueprints.

Without a huge amount of effort, computer-aided design (CAD) now allows you to generate highly realistic three-dimensional (3D) renderings and animations that can demonstrate your dream in action from any angle. You can do cutaways or exploded views (meaning that you can see all the parts, not the after-effects of a bomb), or you can virtually drop the product into any backdrop you like—an Italian piazza or the Grand Canyon.

Even better, soon you will be able to match the production values of an auto show concept car display with 3D holograms that convey the same information at a fraction of the cost. I've seen a prototype of this at Dassault Systèmes.

Today, there is no end to what you can do with a persuasively realistic concept rendering: Use it as a lure for venture capital or crowdfunding on Kickstarter, or test various iterations on prospective customers to see if they might bite on the real thing.

To my mind, the most inspiring example of what's possible is what Alex Andon managed to do with jellyfish tanks. It's a story that's been told before, but I just love this, so I'm going to tell it again.

A marine biologist, Alex wanted to get into the business of selling jellyfish and the special aquariums they need to survive in captivity (in conventional tanks they get sucked down the filters). But who even knew you could keep jellyfish? Until 20 years ago, it wasn't even possible. Consequently, there was absolutely no demand for jellyfish tanks. Alex, age 27, figured he could make and sell them profitably for about $350, but he didn't have the resources to manufacture enough of them to get the ball rolling.

What happened next still amazes me.

Alex made a video of his jellyfish in their tanks and narrated it with an explanation of his dream to manufacture and sell them. In the summer of 2011 he posted this video on Kickstarter, the crowdfunding site on which inventors can pitch their concepts. If members of the online audience are impressed, they can pledge to buy the product if enough orders come in to meet the funding target by a set deadline.

In just 35 days, Alex raised $162,917 from 55 backers, more than enough for an initial production run. In the process he generated widespread media attention that triggered a wave of demand for jellyfish and jellyfish tanks sold through his e-commerce site.

Only in America!

There was nothing "virtual" about Alex's concept presentation; it was basically a home video. But to me it shows the exciting possibilities of combining virtual prototypes with social media. Before it even exists physically, you can make a very detailed animation showing how your design can be used and get it in front of thousands of people.

With a bit more work than Alex did, you can even create a video game–like environment and ask your prospective customer to explore it. For example, in a virtual supermarket, you can ask a shopper to search for items on a shopping list and see if the person's eye happens to land on the product you are working on. What is the shopper's reaction when he or she notices it? What happens if you put it in a different package or change the information on the label?

Virtual prototyping now affords enormous scope for design research from a very early stage. And if you already have advanced CAD capability, the incremental cost may be negligible. You can harvest a rich stream of stakeholder and customer feedback at every step, starting from the most fundamental questions. Is there a market for this? At what price point?

Amazing new virtual prototyping tools are materializing one after another, catering to the challenges posed by specific materials—such as sheet metal—or specific industries.

For instance, an Israeli outfit called Optitex offers a virtual prototyping platform for apparel that allows users to not only accurately render fabric color and texture but also show how frills should look and how the cloth should drape across a model's shoulders. And you can add whatever buttons and trim you like. This makes it easy for a designer in New York to show a manufacturer in Bangladesh exactly how a garment should look, without having to fly samples halfway around the world.

Links like that illustrate the really crucial aspect of virtual prototyping: collaboration. As Nate Siress and his team at Auto Metal Craft in Detroit have discovered (see the feature that follows), there is a huge advantage in having very detailed virtual prototypes—that everyone can see.

Auto Metal Craft prototypes instrument panels for cars, an incredibly complex undertaking in which detail is everything and where many stakeholders are involved. Until recently, few of those details were apparent—and no one except the engineers could even see them—until an expensive and time-consuming physical prototype had been built. To use a golf analogy, many strokes were required to even get close to the green.

Now Auto Metal Craft's virtual prototypes reside in GrabCAD's Workbench cloud-based collaboration tool, which allows everyone involved—even non-CAD users and suppliers and team members on the other side of the world—to go over every millimeter together before anything physical is made. Back to golf again, that means the physical prototype gets built on the green, not off in the rough.

At a certain point, though, even the most zealous CADomaniac must admit there is a limit to what can be achieved virtually. There is no substitute for physical prototypes, preferably hundreds of copies of dozens of iterations. But CAD can take you there, too: issuing precise instructions to a machine that just cranks out a prototype.

Auto Metal Craft: Making It in Motown

Behind the recent renaissance of Detroit's Big Three automakers are dozens if not hundreds of incremental successes achieved by hardworking engineers all over southeast Michigan, people like Nate Siress, chief technology officer at Auto Metal Craft.

Since 1949, Auto Metal Craft has been stamping out prototype parts for the Big Three at its facility in the Detroit suburb of Oak Park. It used to be that most of their work was in sheet metal, but in recent years, one of the company's key specialties has become the highly detailed job of crafting instrument panel prototypes—dashboards and all the many parts they contain.

It is a highly demanding discipline, if only because the dash is the one part of a car that is always within the customer's field of vision and reach. Any ergonomic shortcoming or flaw in fabrication shows up right away—and if it looks or feels cheap, people are immediately turned off.

(continued)

(continued)

"You're dealing with approximately 55 individual parts and assemblies on a metal substructure that needs to give on impact" in the unlikely event of a crash, Nate explains. "So in prototyping, the level of detail is critical for our customers."

Nate has seen a lot of changes in his 33 years with the company, including the introduction of laser-cutting, state-of-the-art resistance welding, and all sorts of mechanical assembly methods. But 3D CAD has become one of his favorite innovations.

"Today, we offer CAD service to provide a lot of design assistance and engineering support," Nate says. "And the changes 3D CAD has brought to the way we interact with our customers are truly monumental."

The process has changed right from the quoting stage. As Nate says: "CAD gives us the ability to send quotes and respond in a timely fashion. We are supplied preliminary data and get back to the customer with a quote. The new technology has sped up this aspect of the prototyping cycle."

For Auto Metal Craft's sales staff, GrabCAD's Workbench has become the go-to tool. "This is the best thing for sales," Nate says. "Most salesmen cannot look at CAD, as it's buried under menus and requires significant training to become proficient." Now, thanks to Workbench, sales staff can learn in minutes how to look at a job in all its complexity and go over the details with customers. "This makes quoting far more accurate, no small factor in the process," Nate adds.

Once a job is under way, Nate says Workbench goes even further in enabling collaboration: "During the iterative process of developing a prototype, there are some changes that may seem small but can, in fact, have a significant impact on the project. With CAD tools, we can see the most current iteration in Workbench, flag it, and factor it into the costing of the prototype and other factors involving such changes."

In a very real sense, Workbench has allowed Auto Metal Craft and its clients to form a unified team, one that can include whoever is needed whenever that person is needed. Instead of crafting custom demos for each meeting, company staff can now just focus everyone's attention on the work in progress. "This is a very major advancement for us," Nate says. "Now, we see everything up front."

The benefits of improved communication throughout the process cannot be overstated; he adds: "Everybody can better visualize the changes from one draft to another, and we can spot potential disasters in the making."

Looking to the future, Nate sees Workbench as a harbinger of positive change: "This is the first step in the right direction. But I look forward to the day when all CAD systems will be in the cloud. This will positively impact our business by eliminating the need to manage CAD software on our internal network, a task that currently requires a significant chunk of time and tremendous cost."

. . . But We Still Need to Get Physical

Three-dimensional printers are fantastic. I have one on my desk, and I love to play with it, feeding it CAD files and watching it methodically add layer upon layer of plastic until the object begins to take on a recognizable shape.

These remarkable devices are still in their infancy, and they are bound to get way, way better at producing more complex forms and working with a wider range of materials. But they are what my friend, manufacturing guru Nick Pinkston, calls a gateway drug, introducing people to the unfolding revolution in product design and manufacturing. All of which is good and useful, but . . .

There has been a lot of hype about how 3D printing is going to magically take manufacturing back to the corner blacksmith's shop, so that everything will be made locally. It's a nice dream for locavores, but it's not going to happen.

One thing that 3D printing likely will do is support fast, inexpensive production of niche and custom items in ways that have not previously been possible. Already we're seeing applications like custom dentures and prosthetic devices. But for production on any kind of scale beyond one-off, better tools are available—and increasingly these can take instructions directly from CAD. What's more, additive processes such as 3D printing don't always deliver what you want from the materials, for instance, the required rigidity or flexibility.

What's really and truly exciting about 3D printers is the new capability they give us to make prototypes directly or to make molds that can be used to fabricate a prototype. This solves some major problems that have bedeviled manufacturers since the dawn of mass production.

Until now, prototypes have been so time-consuming and expensive to make that you didn't want to build one until the very end of the process, not before reaching the point you thought the design was perfect. Even then, as mentioned, because it was so rare and valuable you didn't really want to stress test your prototype—or even let anyone touch it.

With today's new tools—3D printers being one—it is now more and more viable, from early on in the design process, to do many rapid iterations, quickly and cheaply churning out one or two units of variant after variant to see where the bugs are.

The three MIT grads behind Rest Devices (see the feature that follows) discovered just how much you can do these days in-house and on a shoestring budget. They used a MakerBot and hobby kit electronics to turn out more than 100 prototype iterations of Mimo, their amazing baby monitor, in less than 12 months.

Rest Devices: Prototyping Parental Peace-of-Mind

It is every parent's nightmare: that something hideous could happen to your infant child while you are asleep . . . or just down in the kitchen making tea. And when you are studying up before the birth of your first child, reading passages like this one from kidshealth.org are more chilling than anything ever written by Stephen King:

A lack of answers is part of what makes sudden infant death syndrome (SIDS) so frightening.

(*continued*)

(*continued*)

SIDS is the leading cause of death among infants 1 month to 1 year old, and claims the lives of about 2,500 each year in the United States. It remains unpredictable despite years of research.

The worst part of it for parents must be the guilt loop that starts with, "If only I had . . ."

Thanks to a start-up founded by three MIT graduates, there is now a way to address this horrible fear up front.* Mimo is an organic cotton baby body suit equipped with noncontact, machine-washable sensors and a molded "Turtle" encasement for a device that monitors a baby's respiration, activity level, skin temperature, and body position. All this information is transmitted to the Mimo Base Station via Bluetooth.

Boston-based Rest Devices started out in 2011 to develop sensors for a variety of medical applications. "Soon, parents started asking us if they could use our sensors to monitor their baby's breathing," says chief executive officer (CEO) Dulcie Madden. "That changed everything."

In the fall of 2012, starting with a rough idea, Dulcie and cofounders Carson Darling and Thomas Lipoma began to focus their efforts on developing a state-of-the-art baby monitor for the consumer market.

---

*The folks at Rest Devices are careful to make no claim that Mimo in any way prevents SIDS, as to do so would require approval by the U.S. Food and Drug Administration. So the inference here is entirely mine, not Rest Devices'. Parents can make up their own minds.

Just one year later, the result is ready to go on sale around the world at the end of 2013. With Mimo, Dulcie explains, "parents can now monitor their baby's sleep from anywhere."

Rest Devices was able to take Mimo from concept to crib in just 12 months thanks to recent advances in rapid and inexpensive prototyping that allowed everything to be done in-house. "This is an exciting time," says Carson. "There is a big mind shift in hardware, prototyping, and manufacturing. Software development is bringing that to the physical product side."

Carson explains Rest Devices' approach: "We were looking at placing a device on babies, so the question became, 'What is the smallest unit we can build?' We envisioned a simple respiration sensor to link the parent to the baby and give them real-time information via a user-friendly monitor."

The first step was to create a demonstration of the concept; the second was to craft the biometric sensors, the electronics, and the textiles; and the third was to solicit feedback on the resulting prototype from experts and parents.

Rest Devices started by purchasing a 3D printer, the MakerBot Thing-O-Matic. "We designed the product and the molds in CAD, so we could print complete 'Turtles,' the cases for our sensors," Carson says. Then the team acquired an injection-molding machine, created a surface mount soldering area in the shop, and designed a custom PCB printing and etching tank.

(continued)

(continued)

"Since the core of this project was electronics, to rapidly design a circuit and test it on the same day became important to us," Carson says. But ordering a custom board for next-day delivery would have cost $1,200, a prohibitively high tab. "The cost to do a rougher version in-house is far less, and we could do three or four iterations in two days."

The ability to keep prototyping in-house was invaluable. Carson says: "We could see what was going to work. We could experiment a lot more, iterating constantly."

The result was an initial prototype just seven and a half weeks out from concept stage, a fully functioning unit that the team was able to test with families. That testing yielded valuable data. Among other lessons, the team learned that the basic version of their Turtle was too high and too big for the baby and that the look and feel of the final product was a key feature for discerning parents. "With feedback from parents," explains Dulcie, "we were able to move forward and refine the prototype."

The Wi-Fi end-user experience was also critical. The team wanted to be sure the information parents received on their computers or smartphones came with a reassuringly intuitive and visually pleasing aesthetic, rather than a clinical readout.

"As well, we learned that to get the right kind of feedback from parents, who were very particular about what they put next to their baby, our prototypes had to look and feel complete," says Dulcie.

The ability to do many iterations meant that parents were able to vet all aspects of the design every step of the way. "Clear feedback from our end users was important to us throughout the development process," says Dulcie. "This feedback shaped our final product, and in the end, it was surprising how little money we spent on each iteration."

"Developing our Turtle in a lab would have cost $6,000 to $8,000 per mold," adds Carson. "Our cost was just $200 to $400."

After crafting a hundred or more Turtles with MakerBot plus many more iterations of the electronics, and being guided by continuous feedback from parents, less than a year later Mimo was ready for production and marketing.

From this experience, what lessons does Carson have to offer other hardware start-ups?

"Get the laser cutter and 3D printer, and make use of injection molding," he advises. "With these devices, you can think of something and have it right away. These prototyping tools tear down the walls, foster collaboration, and make iteration faster. You don't have to wait until it is perfect."

When we interviewed the Rest Devices team in the fall of 2013, Mimo was nearly ready to go on sale around the world, thanks to a distribution deal with a major

(continued)

(*continued*)

global retailer. "We sealed the deal with really cool consumer packaging," says Dulcie. "And, of course, we did
all the iterations in-house, with feedback from the parents
on the packaging and branding."

Critically, Rest Devices' later-stage prototypes had to feel
pristine and complete before parents would even consider putting them on their sleeping infants. But the feedback from that
real-world experience was invaluable in helping the team go
from concept to global market in less than a year—for a fraction
of what it would have cost a major manufacturer.

Not that the big boys have failed to notice the utility of
rapid iteration. Nowhere is it more critical than where the task
is to design an object in a standard size but make it fit perfectly
with something that is anything but standard—like a shoe and
the human foot.

So it is no surprise to find that both Nike and Adidas, the
sports shoe giants, are among the leaders in using 3D printing
for rapid prototyping. As reported by the *Financial Times*, 3D
printing has enabled Adidas to slash the prototyping cycle from
four to six weeks down to one or two days. Similarly, Nike was
able to do 12 fully tested prototype rounds in six months as it
developed a new line of shoes for American football players.
I guess that's what they mean by "Just do it."

And nowadays there are several ways you can do it, too.

As we saw in the previous chapter, if you have a brilliant idea
but lack the skills and resources needed to take it—virtually or
physically—through design and prototype, you can take it to

the team at Quirky, which has a cutting-edge rapid prototyping shop. Or, as discussed earlier in this chapter, you can seek backing for your idea from Kickstarter and prototype it yourself as the folks at Rest Devices did. But what if you virtually prototyped your dream in 3D CAD and you have—at a carefully modulated, investor-sanctioned rate—some cash to burn? As the Ghostbusters put it, "Who you gonna call?"

Answer: An outfit like Fathom in Oakland, California (see the feature that follows), or one of the other rapid prototyping specialists beginning to sprout around the world, that's who. What Fathom offers is a full suite of the latest prototyping tools—3D printers and much more—plus the CAD and tooling expertise needed bring them together seamlessly. For a large company the cost for this service will probably look like a steal; maybe less so for seat-of-the-pants inventors.

Which route is best? The answer depends very much on the complexity of your product, how much skill you have in your hands, and how much cash you have in your pocket. The ideal is probably to do as much as you can in-house—both to learn and minimize cash burn—and turn to suppliers such as Fathom at critical points in the process.

Fathom: Deep into Prototyping

"It's an exciting time to get in the prototyping game," says Tony Slavik, studio manager at Fathom, an Oakland, California-based rapid-prototyping specialist that supports inventors in the San Francisco Bay Area. And he's

(continued)

(continued)

right, because specialist outlets such as Fathom are still rare—even in a territory where cutting-edge inventors are thick on the ground.

Opening their doors in 2008, Fathom founders Rich Stump and Michelle Mihevc caught the maker wave at precisely the right moment. When I first went to the Bay Area in 2010, "hardware" was still nowhere on the radar and most people looked bored when the word was mentioned. So Fathom was truly prescient.

How big is the wave that Fathom is now surfing? When *Inc.* magazine's September 2013 issue featured a list of America's 500 fastest-growing companies, Fathom clocked in at 369. Just to make the 500 cut, a company needed a sales growth speed in excess of 918.59 percent.

So, yeah, I think we can agree with Tony.

Fathom's winning formula is to be totally plug-compatible with 3D CAD creators, offering all the tooling needed to render a physical prototype from a virtual design, fast, affordably, and backed by leading-edge expertise.

"Today's tools to help customers create mechanical physical objects are amazing," Tony says. "People come to Fathom in a hurry, eager to have their prototypes in hand . . . it's the ultimate testing ground. With the latest technologies—like 3D CAD services, 3D printing, additive manufacturing, and model finishing—we're able to deliver an accurate preview of that final product, complete with the aesthetics, materials, and functionality."

For Tony and his team, the key to the process is close collaboration with the clients, whose needs range from simple to highly iterative and complex.

"Prototyping is a huge step, the foray into making a design real, stepping into real life. Many of our customers come to us with CAD prototype files that require additional work," Tony says. "We know what to look for and how to help our customers arrive at the kinds of changes that will facilitate the prototype's production or add to a design's strength and its ability to be produced."

Once the design has been optimized for Fathom's tooling, the next stages are largely automated.

"For project designs in 3D CAD, our technology is a dream come true," Tony says. "For the most part, it runs unattended. We just set up the processes and start the machines. After that, the parts are built and in the end there it is, a functional prototype."

To achieve that kind of seamless process, Fathom has invested in some of the most advanced additive manufacturing technologies on the market, including fused deposition modeling (FDM), selective laser sintering (SLS), and direct metal laser sintering (DMLS). Fathom has also hired people with the expertise needed to drive the tools to the max.

Prototyping is the marquee specialty, but Fathom also builds parts in short runs. "Print for manufacture is an exciting option for small-scale production runs," Tony

(*continued*)

(continued)

says. "These technologies are changing the rules of scale for some manufacturers. This is and will continue to be very good for many industries and makers."

Tony sees similar changes ahead in the scale required for success in rapid prototyping. As a pioneer, Fathom has had to make a significant investment in tooling that's as high cost as it is high tech. But Tony expects capital costs to decline as sophisticated tooling proliferates and as patents expire on key technologies.

"The status quo is changing, for certain," Tony says. "In the very near future, a number of patents will be expiring for laser sintering, which is used for some of the most advanced printers that can create parts in anything from nylon to titanium. So we could see a major drop in prices further down the line."

At the same time plenty of challenges and much scope for improvement remain. "We're always pushing the limitations of the technologies," Tony says. "Injection molds are challenging, and materials can be a real challenge." One critical need is for heat-defusing strategies to mitigate temperature boundaries during the fabrication of a part. "But these limitations will fade as the technology becomes more refined," he adds.

Upstream, meanwhile, Tony says he is confident that continuing advances in 3D CAD "will even further enable creators and makers to visualize and turn their ideas into reality." I'd say he's right on that score, too.

Where outside help may be most valuable is at the end of the process, when you need a highly polished prototype to put in the hands of prospective customers. In fact, ideally you want dozens to hundreds of units that you can put in the hands of consumers and distributors . . . marketing samples, lots of them.

It is high time to do that because—insanely—many companies are still committing to incredibly costly mass-production programs without really knowing if they have something consumers actually want but praying that they do. In effect, it's a form of gambling with shareholders' money.

So at the end of the prototyping process, ideally, you want the ability to affordably build a short run that can be given to target consumers to use intensively. And maybe you want a selection of styles and colors to see which one they prefer. If you're making airliners, of course, that won't be possible. For anything less complex, let the customers experience the product and see how they like it. Find out if there are any glitches that your team failed to consider. Are there parts a small child could swallow? (This is currently a front-of-mind issue in my own household.)

Suppliers such as Fathom already offer a certain level of short-run production capability, but at this point, you may want to look over the horizon, simply because prototyping on this scale may not be a need that 3D printing can fill economically. The good news is that a growing universe of other flexible, numerically controlled machine tools is steadily bringing down the cost of small-lot production.

CAD in the cloud supports this with the ability to directly instruct flexible tooling with a minimum of expensive and time-consuming setup processes: Just load the file and press Start.

That makes it much easier to work with prototyping suppliers anywhere on the planet. When sourcing prototype or short-run production, it's worth shopping around. An order that might be too small for a U.S. supplier to consider may be a plum job for someone in a small market like New Zealand . . . or Estonia. (Since Estonia's president wrote a blurb for this book, I'll take this opportunity to promote investment.)

Again, it's about convergence driving change. An emerging culture of open networking meets new and powerful cloud tools meets new virtual and physical rendering tools.

How disruptive is this likely to be? Look again at the example of Rest Devices. Three young engineers, without a lot of funding or fancy equipment, were able to take a very innovative product from rough idea to global markets in just 12 months. To do it, they had to navigate an incredibly tricky customer prototyping process: getting mothers to give them access to their newborns. Where would most large companies be 12 months out from a rough idea like this? They would still be talking about it. Or actually, in America, the lawyers would be reviewing it.

In prototyping, as historic obstacles fall by the wayside, there are few limits left in the way of ingenuity. And, as we'll see in the next chapter, it's a similar story in manufacturing.

Executive Takeaways

Manufacturers typically have a well-defined product development process. In the service sector, on the other hand, the process of developing new customer offerings tends to be less clear-cut.

- If your business isn't manufacturing, what is your equivalent of prototyping?

- How do you test an idea before you fully develop it?

- What new technologies or approaches would allow you to lower the cost of that testing process by a factor of 10 or to slash the time required down to one-tenth the current level while incorporating a richer stream of customer feedback?

7 Manufacturing

Here You Go; Make This

At the end of the day, it's all about manufacturing. No matter how brilliantly conceived your design is, no matter how cool it looks in a computer-aided design (CAD) program, if you can't make it on quality, on time, and within budget, it's just taking up space on a server.

So how will the revolution in product design and development play out on the factory floor? Will open engineering add momentum to the march toward outsourcing and offshoring, pushing even more manufacturing activity to China? Or will it draw product development and manufacturing closer together? Will it be the catalyst to a manufacturing renaissance in the rich world? And will it tilt the playing field toward agile upstarts and away from giant corporations?

All these outcomes and more are possible as new design tools and a newly empowered engineering culture converge with rapid innovations in factory automation. Right *now*, the deck of cards is being reshuffled. And when the next hands are dealt, odds are that everything we take for granted about the advantages of scale and location in manufacturing will be reordered. That is not to say we can predict any outcome with certainty because, as in poker, it's not the hand that you're dealt; it's how you play your cards.

Or as my friend, manufacturing guru Nick Pinkston puts it (see the feature that follows), the changes now under way do not decisively push manufacturing in any specific direction. Instead, they put it on wheels, making it more viable wherever customers and creators want it.

With those caveats up front, we can point to several clearly evident and converging trends.

Manufacturing in the Nick of Time

My friend Nick Pinkston is what you might call a manufacturing guru, a visionary who sees over the horizon to a new and very different production ecosystem. He's originally from Pittsburgh, in what used to be America's metal-bashing heartland. But these days you will find him in San Francisco, where he is in the thick of the maker's movement. It's an intense scene that is generating growing momentum toward a renaissance in American manufacturing, but this time with a more artisanal focus on craftsmanship.

Whereas I am an upstream guy, focused on collaborative design in the cloud, Nick has both feet on the factory floor—and I am fascinated by what he sees. So I drink his Kool-Aid every chance I get, and I am happy to serve some to you by way of a condensed version of some of the things he has told me.

Q: So what is driving change in manufacturing? Is it all about three-dimensional (3D) printing?

A: "Hardware is the new software." That is to say, hardware today is where software was around 40 years ago. In fact, very little has changed over the past 100 years in traditional manufacturing. It's like the massive mainframe computers back in the day, with the legions of programmers and operators required to run them, but everything is changing. The mixing of computers with manufacturing technology—this is where the change lies, and where the real work is to be done.

What drove innovation in software is now being reapplied to manufacturing. While the tools won't change that much, the trends that will drive change in manufacturing are largely technological. In a nutshell, the digitization of manufacturing is the new Industrial Revolution. APIs [application programming interfaces] will use computers to perform and control many of the functions on the factory floor . . . effectively doing things that now require human labor, not only relatively unskilled, but also highly skilled. At the moment, people do these things better than machines, but this is changing fast. One way I like to describe the future of the factory floor is this: Envision the mentality of a 3D printer as the coming model for manufacturing.

3D printing is like a gateway drug in that it gets people into this, but it's just one of many key technologies here. The real story is two trends that are going to completely change manufacturing: a new generation of numerically controlled tools—3D printing being just one—and a new universe of expert software that will give the designer/creator all the skills that

(*continued*)

(*continued*)

used to reside on the factory floor or in the purchasing department.

Q: How does all this link up with 3D CAD, which is at the design end of this revolution?

A: 3D CAD is the perfect IDE [integrated developer environment] interface between design and manufacturing . . . where everything can be gathered and contained, simulated, and checked for bugs. In the future I envision CAD as being able to contain specifics—like "give me these bolts and those custom components"—combining many functions that now require separate programs, into one 3D CAD file. I see 3D CAD as increasing its expressivity.

3D CAD that further empowers engineers and designers, and eliminates intermediaries on the factory floor, and enables greater expressivity—that's the way of the future.

Q: We can see that all these changes, from concept through to the factory, are going to completely reshuffle the deck and reorder the whole matrix of factors in the manufacturing equation. So let's break it down and look at it factor by factor. To start off, what's all this going to do to "scale"?

A: Scale is going to move both ways. In engineering, there's the old adage: "Good, fast, cheap—pick two." As product design and innovation speed up, this becomes more competitive for everyone. Economies of scale are important and always will be, but with increased automation, smaller scale becomes not only possible but also economically viable. And that fits the reality of the modern consumer, who wants the newest, the best, and the latest.

Q: Okay, how about flexibility and speed? From the design end, we are now able to prototype rapidly and introduce and variants just as fast. How will the new manufacturing technologies amplify this? Is the competitive focus going to shift the speed to market?

A: The entire product cycle is certainly getting faster and will continue to do so. With design and prototyping revolutionized by technology, certainly the ability to meet consumers' rising expectations will only increase. Now, with smaller entrants to the marketplace equipped with the same CAD tools as the big players, competition is going to increase.

One place that new competition is going to come from is crowdfunding. Until very recently, it has been impossible to think about developing and manufacturing a product without massive fund-raising. One successful example so far is the Pebble, a smart watch that displays notifications from smartphones and offers a range of apps. It was developed by niche technology start-up Pebble Technology, funded through Kickstarter, and began shipping in January 2013. Now dozens of companies are scrambling to bring a smart watch to market.

(continued)

(continued)

The broader trend here is the highly competitive nature of today's marketplace and the focus on giving consumers what they want. Technologies that automate manufacturing—and remove or reduce the labor cost factor—may, indeed, push production closer to the consumers. We could see regional manufacturing return, focused on serving the consumer. But it will be manufacturing like it has not been seen before.

Q: What about the question of labor versus technology? Until now there has been a massive shift to low-cost venues. Is the shift to greater reliance on technology going to reverse that?

A: As labor costs get stripped out of the equation—and this is already beginning to happen, with one robot able to replace 50 factory floor workers, including highly skilled ones—U.S. manufacturing is increasingly able to compete with China and other low-cost locations. There is still the human factor to consider: Humans are really good robots. Robot retraining is very costly at present, but rethinking robotics to enable ordinary workers to program them is really going to alter that equation.

Designers are expensive. Creative people are expensive. All engineering is costly. These functions are here to stay, but factory floor labor is going to evolve and, for the most part, seriously diminish if not disappear. R&D and technology jobs are here to stay, but the factory floor of tomorrow is going to look very different.

Q: What about the cost of all this new manufacturing technology? Is it going to be more accessible for smaller players?

A: Digitized manufacturing technologies will allow smaller companies to enter the market—and be competitive. While the cost for machines is going up—and injection molding remains expensive—as labor inputs shrink with automation, the cost per unit is going to be lower. At the same time, "tech sharing" (a good current example of this is Shapeways) will give smaller players access to millions of dollars of equipment—and that will continually enable small companies to enter the market with new products, ramping up the competition for entrenched players.

Q: Do you expect these new players will outsource everything, try to do it themselves? Or is some kind of new model going to emerge?

A: What I like to talk about are hybrid verticals, or new verticals. The most difficult aspect of manufacturing is assembly. Plainly stated, it's hard, and the most challenging part of getting a product to market. New vertical companies may outsource components but assemble their products in-house. This way they maintain control of the quality and speed of manufacturing. They can customize quicker than if they

(continued)

(continued)

have outsourced, and with increased automation they have removed the labor costs of assembly. Companies will always need to weigh their quality and processes against their risks and needs. In some cases, automation will enable companies to be fully integrated, while others will create new ways of manufacturing their products.

Q: What does all this do to locational advantage? Does that push production closer to the customer?

A: Certainly. As labor costs recede with increased automation, manufacturing closer to the customer begins to make more sense; we will no longer be restrained by the labor cost factor. Manufacturing along regional lines, with products designed for specific markets and consumer preferences, is the way of the future. Closer to the customer is better. Responsive to consumer needs is better. A focus on the consumer is a big part of this trend.

Q: Put all of these factors together, and where are we headed? And what, if anything, is holding us back?

A: Traditionally, hardware has been a conservative culture, and engineers a conservative lot. But with the influx of software culture and people moving into the hardware space, a lot of this conservatism will be left behind.

Where does it go? Already, we're seeing crowdfunding change the way new companies are capitalizing

Manufacturing 159

their ventures and bringing products to market. They are going to seriously challenge the traditional players. But my best response here is that we're moving in the direction of serving the consumer, who will increasingly drive manufacturing and change this relationship. Let's look at what happened with the Web: First it was huge companies, and then, over time, the consumer pushed "big" back. I see the future of manufacturing in much the same way. The old "we make, you buy" relationship between the consumer and manufacturer is evolving. In the future, manufacturing will become part of a far richer ecosystem.

No More Colored Collars?

All the way back to the medieval guilds, the process of making things has been ordered by distinctions of trade and class. To leave no room for doubt, the various groups have even dressed differently: collars blue or white; white hard hats for foremen and neckties for bosses; turtlenecks for designers and pocket protectors for engineers. Happily, all this nonsense is starting to disappear.

At the top of the product development process, there has always been a certain division between engineers—aka gearheads—and designers. They may not come from different planets, but they certainly come from different ends of the college campus. The art school aesthetes see the gearheads as beer-swilling barbarians; the gearheads see art school types as . . . well, never mind.

Even long after everyone has outgrown the frat house, the two disciplines have still brought different perspectives to product development. And the gap has been maintained by the fact that each discipline has worked in different tools with little fidelity between them. In stereotype, the designers are all about form, whereas the engineers focus on function. CAD is quickly erasing that distinction by uniting both disciplines with a single tool.

Still, the gap within the office is nothing compared with the huge cultural gulf separating design from the factory. My first encounter with this left my heart pounding.

As a novice engineer at a door maker in Estonia, I served as the liaison with personnel on the factory floor who, not long before, had been jolted out of their relaxed Soviet work style by a new system of piecework pay. The first guy I had to deal with was a big, burly Ukrainian welder who was so strong he would lift elevator cabin frames all by himself. When I approached him to discuss changes to my drawings for the piece he was working on, he came right up in my face and snarled at me the Russian equivalent to, "You little snot. If you make trouble for me, I will beat the living shit out of you."

I was absolutely certain that he was not kidding around.

The same kind of warm, loving relationships have long been a part of manufacturing in the United States as well, entrenched by the divide between labor and management. I've heard that development engineers in Detroit dismissively call their production colleagues "plant rats." Meanwhile, on the factory side, every veteran production engineer has tales from the "bad old days" of idiotic blueprints sent down from the office with no thought about how to build them efficiently. So the critical hand-off from design to production came with little more than a Post-it Note thrown over the factory wall that said, "Here you go; now make this."

The Japanese, with their genius for continuous process improvement, blew this stupid system out of the water by applying methodologies such as design for manufacture (DFM) and design for assembly (DFA). Eventually, American manufacturers were forced to catch up—which, in large part, is why America still has a car industry.

Rigorously prototyped and detailed specs in 3D CAD now make the design-to-manufacturing hand-off much smoother. And that has helped make it possible to outsource production to the other side of the world, across language barriers and day-to-night time zone gaps.

This is one of two contradictory emerging trends. On one side, today's tools enable the near-complete divorce of design (in the United States, Japan, or Europe) and manufacturing (in China or some other low-cost country). On the other side, the very same tools support very tight integration of design and production, both in terms of physical location and collarless social organization.

Offshoring: Amazingly Enough, It Works . . . So Far

These days, as often as not, the people who develop products have never even set eyes on the factories where they are produced or on the workers who actually produce them. Objects designed and engineered in Gothenburg or Chicago are produced half a world away in Guangzhou or Chittagong.

Separating such critically interdependent functions with forbiddingly steep barriers of language and time zones can be, no

surprise, a recipe for disaster. In fact, you could write an ency-
clopedia of offshoring disaster stories: the laugh-out-loud stories
about defects that occur when key instructions get lost in translation and the tales of shipments through a nail-bitingly long
supply chain that didn't arrive till after Christmas. Followed by
the punch line: But the pirated copies of your product were in
stores by Thanksgiving—ha-ha! Or not funny at all: A global
brand is shamed after a shoddy factory collapses on a thousand
women working on the production runs of major retailers from
around the world. And more such stories exist.

It is a measure of how huge the cost advantages of offshoring are that companies are willing to undertake all the risks
involved. Even more, it's a measure of how hard contract manufacturers have worked to smooth kinks in the system to deliver
on quality, on time, and within budget.

Cloud-based CAD tools (like our own Workbench) also
now make it much easier to avoid misunderstandings by allowing both sides to see the same detailed images in real time and
discuss issues by pointing at and sketching on those images
instead of trying to verbalize everything through translators. In
a meeting, it is difficult enough to make yourself understood
in your own language; this is a literal version of that kid's game
telephone.

One critical link in the chain is the availability of specialists such as Boston/Shenzhen-based Dragon Innovation (see the
following feature). Led by seasoned veterans of offshore contract
manufacturing, the Dragon team leads neophyte product developers through the intricate process of writing specification for all
aspects of production and logistics, then seeking and comparing
bids from contractors.

Dragon Innovation: Taking the Hard Out of Hardware

In terms of quality, speed, and above all price, Chinese contract manufacturers have become hard to beat in recent decades, so hard to beat, in fact, that China is now the first resort for product developers from around the world. But with its unfamiliar language, freewheeling business culture, and shaky legal system, China is not a place that is transparent to outsiders—in any sense of that term. This is why, if you want to take the China route, you need well-seasoned guides.

Scott Miller and Herman Pang fit that description to a T. Before founding Boston/Shenzhen-based Dragon Innovation in 2009, the pair racked up years of experience on the front lines of high-volume offshore manufacturing, with projects that included toys for Hasbro and Disney and the Roomba robot vacuum cleaner.

Today, they help American outfits, large and small, navigate the intricacies and pitfalls of offshore production (mainly in China) right from the prototype stage. And they are now moving upstream all the way to crowdfunding the development of new products.

"Hardware is still hard," says Scott, Dragon's chief executive officer (CEO) (Herman is president). "While technology has made product design, prototyping, and getting potential customers excited about the potential of

(*continued*)

(continued)

a new product easier than ever, the road from prototype to consumer-scale finished product remains monumentally challenging."

This is why Dragon is focused on providing start-ups with support from the earliest possible stage. "For product developers, there are a lot of unknowns," Scott says. "There is very little understanding of hardware, inventory, and lead times. We saw an opportunity to provide critical expertise for hardware start-ups, from product development through every phase of the manufacturing process."

Along the way, Dragon helps product developers choose the right manufacturing supplier; source components, materials, and tooling; overcome challenges ranging from regulatory compliance to material shrinkage; and use the logistics needed to get the final product to consumers.

"We've served as the interface between some pretty spectacular ideas and the store shelves," Scott says, pointing to a client list of more than 100 companies, including MakerBot, Sifteo, Pebble, and Romotive.

Dragon's process begins with a careful assessment of each product's design. "The design review capabilities of 3D CAD have had a profound impact on manufacturing," Scott says. "We help our clients use these capabilities to make the manufacturing process a success."

Using CAD tools that support design for manufacture and assembly (DFMA), the team works to identify and eliminate any gaps in the design that could lead to problems on the factory floor. Once the product is ready to move into production, Dragon then helps the client source a factory. "We have over 100 factories in our network—many but not all in China—and work with 20 to 30 factories on a regular basis," Scott says.

At this point, clients often make an initial trip to China, visiting factories to gauge factors like the fit and accessibility of management and track record for producing similar products and to tap into word of mouth from other clients. "From there we choose three to five and begin the RFQ [request for quotation] process," Scott says.

Prior to this stage, Dragon prepares a bill of materials, with a full breakdown of cost and cycle time, capturing and itemizing every input, including factory margins, labor rates, and other related costs. This allows clients to see everything, including the details of factory-sourced component costs. So when the quotes come in, they get an accurate apples-to-apples comparison from every potential factory.

"This is a highly detailed and critical step in the process," Scott says. "You want to avoid unexpected costs, such as scrap charges at the end of the job, so the bill of materials should guarantee no hidden costs or surprises."

From there, Dragon and the client make a shortlist of potential factories before sitting down to negotiate cost savings and payment terms. If all goes well, a final commitment is made. Once a contract has been signed, Dragon brings the client's engineering team to China (or

(continued)

(continued)

wherever the factory may be) to work out any final design changes face to face.

"This is when the relationship between our clients and their factory begins to cement," Scott says. The visitors can then go home knowing that Dragon will monitor the job closely to ensure top quality. For Scott and the entire Dragon team, that's the main goal. "Quality is critical," he says. "You want to deliver customer satisfaction—performance that meets consumer expectations, on time and within budget."

Still, the goalposts are moving. So with an eye to the changes in the product development and manufacturing ecosystem at the heart of this book, Dragon is shifting its focus upstream and closer to home. In the fall of 2013, the company launched a crowdfunding platform aimed at allowing hardware start-ups to make the leap from prototype to production. Scott sees this as the wave of the future, a future where he expects manufacturing to happen closer to home and in smaller lots of 1,000 to 5,000 units. "This volume is best suited for domestic manufacturing," Scott says, "so that the entrepreneur can be close to the contract manufacturer and provide high-bandwidth feedback with minimal lag time."

What's more, over the next 5 to 10 years, Scott expects to see a manufacturing revolution in America, based on small-lot production using advanced additive manufacturing technologies.

In this way, the people at Dragon Innovation have the bases covered, taking the *hard* out of *hardware* all the way from China to Chicago.

You can do it on your own, of course, by checking prices and sending out requests for quotation (RFQs) on sites such as Alibaba.com. But what you get is *not* some off-the-shelf commodity. Factory owners are real people, warts and all, who deal day in, day out with their own specific issues: "Someone hired away all the people who know how to operate that machine" or "Material of that type sold here is bad quality at high price," for example. And guess what? Not everyone is trustworthy. Unless you are Apple with enough resources to comb through every facet of Foxconn's operations, it's a black box.

Yet, amazingly perhaps, contracting out to China seems to work—and for several reasons beyond low wage rates. Regions such as Guangdong, inland from Hong Kong, now have a phenomenal base of suppliers and subcontractors who compete fiercely on speed and price.

What's more, shipping products from China is cheap, probably cheaper than most people realize.

The newest container ships can carry more than 10,000 TEUs (twenty-foot equivalent units), which equals 5,000 tractor-trailers, each hauling a 40-foot container. And they do it with just a couple of dozen crew, mostly at low wages. The big expense—roughly half the operating cost—is fuel. At the top speed of 25 knots (just under 29 miles per hour), one of these behemoths can make the 6,500-nautical-mile voyage from Hong Kong to Los Angeles in 11 days. But at that speed, they burn on average 350 tons of bunker fuel a day, which costs (at mid-2013 rates that average $650/ton) about $2.5 million over the voyage. If that seems like a lot, it is still just $500 per 40-foot container. Double that amount, and you get an idea of the vessel's overall base operating cost per container: $1,000 . . . at top speed.

High fuel costs, however, have incented shipping companies to slow down and save big. At 17 knots, it takes the largest container ships an extra five days (16 versus 11) to travel from Hong Kong to Los Angeles—but instead of burning 350 tons of fuel a day, they burn just 100 tons. That slashes the fuel bill from $2.5 million down to just over $1 million, or just $200 per 40-foot container. Port handling charges, inspection fees, and margins for many hands along the way boosts that significantly.

Bottom line is that all-in, you can still get a 40-foot container shipped door to door, Shenzhen to Los Angeles, for about $2,000. These days it just takes a week longer. By contrast, trucking out from Los Angeles, for the same price, you can get the same container only as far as Albuquerque, New Mexico (800 miles at the 2013 average rate of $2.55 per mile).

For not much more than freight rates to the West Coast, you can ship directly from China to ports along the Gulf of Mexico and the Eastern seaboard—and when the Panama Canal expansion opens in 2015, larger vessels are expected to mean lower rates.

This is the reality of globalization. Any location close to a major container port has a significant logistical advantage over landlocked cities in the middle of continents. So transport *cost* is not going to erode China's competitive edge any time soon.

The flip side is the time it takes to ship—now a week longer as shippers shift to "slow steaming." Adding a month or more to the lag time between order and delivery has big downsides.

Having precisely the right amount of inventory on hand a month before Christmas is, in many businesses, the pivot point between profit and loss. Overorder and you end up trying to cut your losses by dumping product in postholiday sales, thereby diminishing your future pricing power. Underorder and you may leave the lion's share of your profit unharvested.

Either way you lose. So it can be a decisive advantage if your "elves" can deliver a rush production run—in maybe two weeks—once you see how orders are shaping up in the critical week somewhere around the end of November. You might get that in China, but the cost of airfreight—if you can find space at that time of year—is prohibitive unless you are making silk scarves or something.

If that begins to nudge the scale away from China, what's really beginning to make it tip is the steady erosion of the edge that drew American business over there in the first place: low labor costs. With steeply rising wage rates and a strengthening currency, a 2013 study by AlixPartners predicts that China's manufacturing costs will be on par with those of the United States by 2015.

There is a demographic inevitability to this trend as the effects of China's one-child policy reach into a new generation. Since the one-child law came into effect in 1979, there are now few second children in China younger than age 35. As the larger pre-1979 cohort—the backbone of Chinese factory labor—gradually moves into middle age, there will be fewer younger workers to replace them.

Then there is the "brain drain." China produces masses of very smart, well-educated engineers. But because of the hardships of life in the People's Republic—choking air pollution and worries about food safety topping the list—the best and brightest typically leap at any chance to emigrate. The same pressures make it tough to get expats to accept a long-term posting in China.

All this has prompted many businesses to consider new low-cost locations, such as India and Indonesia. But those countries entail new hurdles, and they lack the huge efficiencies of China's supplier clusters and massive logistical throughput.

Give the Chinese credit: They're not just cheap; they are now very good at what they do, and they will be a formidable force in global manufacturing from here on. More and more, they will begin making their own products.

So where is the next "paradise" for manufacturers? It may be closer to the customers . . . or right under your nose where you can make sure the job is being done right.

Homemade: Now It Just May Be Viable

Yes, it is now entirely possible to divorce design from manufacturing and have everything made on the other side of the world. No matter how seamless you make the process, though, as the product creator you still lose something when you are not integrally involved in its manufacture, starting with opportunities for continuous learning and hands-on control of inventory and quality.

When you are in and out of the factory on a daily basis, you have a real-time awareness of the process. The people doing it give you get feedback. You can see the error rates from each machine. You know the cost of each step down to the last penny. As all this infiltrates your imagination, you tend to recognize opportunities for improvement.

What makes even more sense—call it a no-brainer—is to build as close to your customers as possible. As noted previously, the key to sustained profit is the ability to respond to fluctuating demand rapidly and, equally important, *precisely*. You don't want to build more than you can sell or less than you could sell. Forget trying to design algorithms to predict what mix of colors and sizes people will want six months from now; if you want to win, make this week what's needed on the shelf next week.

If you are in Europe and your customers are also in Europe, it would seem to make sense to manufacture there, unless there is some huge factor weighing in the other direction. Until now, that factor has been China's highly motivated, low-cost labor. But as we saw with Zara, the Spanish apparel chain, the balance between low labor cost and speed to market is definitely open to debate.

Here is where the reshuffle kicks in. Just as the playing field seems to be shifting away from long supply chains, a new universe of hard and soft tooling is emerging to radically reorder all the equations of manufacturing: scale, speed, location advantage, ratio of labor to technology, flexibility, capital cost, barriers to entry, and marketing of production capacity.

This may well mean the tables get turned. Big may have less advantage over small but nimble. Far but cheap may lose ground to fast and smart on the spot. Manufacturing activity may start to migrate back to North America and Europe.

But just in case you are starting to feel sorry for the Chinese at this point, look what they are left with: the customers *they* are closest to. Within a 4,000-kilometer (2,500-mile) radius of Hong Kong, which is roughly the distance from New York to Los Angeles or Lisbon to Moscow, they have all of China, Japan, Korea, Southeast Asia, Bangladesh, and most of India. That's more than 3 billion people, half of humanity, in the world's fastest-growing markets. So if your aspirations are global, it is likely that you will still need to manufacture in China or its neighborhood.

Enough about China, though. It's time to meet Baxter.

Robots That Speak CAD

For at least the past 40 years, robots have been hailed (and reviled) as the wave of a future that never seemed to arrive. They were going to revolutionize factory work and steal everyone's job, but like room-temperature superconductors and fuel cells, they never seemed to live up to their hype. Sure, we've all seen car factory footage of welding robots surrounded by showers of sparks, but has Rosey the Robot ever brought you a coffee like she used to do for George Jetson?

No, and that's because robots, for all their promise, have been wickedly expensive and less flexible than a militant factory shop steward. Try telling a million-dollar welding robot to pick up the litter around its workstation. It won't even bother to say, "Fuggedaboutit; that's not in my job description." It will just ignore you. Until now, teaching a robot to do new tricks has taken weeks of work by specialized code jockeys. And although robots are fast, they are dangerous unless caged where they can't whack human colleagues on the head. For all their logical inconsistencies, humans have proved cheaper, smarter, and more flexible—that is, until Baxter came along.

Billed by his proud parents, Boston-based Rethink Robotics, as "the world's first common sense interactive factory robot," Baxter is revolutionary on several fronts. Like a demented elf on crystal meth, he will work three shifts every day through the pre-Christmas rush doing repetitive tasks such as loading and unloading machines, sorting parts, and packing boxes. But he will never "break bad" and hurt his colleagues. Thanks to an ingenious system of 360-degree sensors, Baxter can work elbow-to-elbow with humans. In fact, unskilled coworkers can teach him to do new tasks, quickly and simply, just by moving his arms through a series of new moves.

What is really revolutionary is that Baxter sells for just $22,000—less than the one-year cost of a minimum-wage employee in America—a price point within range of any small manufacturing outfit. Twenty years ago, that would have prompted fears that Baxter would steal jobs. Today, people realize he can help bring jobs back from China, by doing repetitive tasks that Americans shun anyway.

Baxter could be the poster bot for the changes now under way in manufacturing. Like 3D printing, though, he is just one piece of a much larger puzzle. Every piece of machinery in the factory—lathes, presses, injection-molding equipment, what have you—is on its way to getting intelligence and the ability to communicate by receiving instructions electronically and reporting its status. In what language will this communication happen? In the computer code of CAD, of course.

Cloud-based CAD is going to create a seamless chain of communication from the screens of creators and marketers all the way to Baxter's "fingertips." With this will come a comprehensive, real-time awareness of the process from end to end. How is that different from what we have today?

As things stand, to an unreasonable degree, outsourced manufacturing is a black box. Okay, so you may never learn enough Cantonese to communicate with the woman in Guangdong who is processing your order, but there is no reason why you shouldn't be able to talk to the machine she operates, remotely monitoring its performance in real time—and instructing it. Not only can you not do that, Nick Pinkston tells me that contract manufacturers in China generally don't even directly run the CAD files they get from clients. They use what they are given to build their own files—and they keep those, thank you very much.

How come the black box is on your end, anyway? Wouldn't it be better to keep your intellectual property close to your chest and send encrypted instructions to your contractor's machines?

The Earth Becomes Flat

From one side, the labor cost differential between the advanced and emerging economies is becoming less and less of a steep slope. From the other side, labor's share of total manufacturing cost is set to decline as new technology does more and more of the work. That new technology—for example, Baxter—is much more affordable for smaller players and geared to producing flexibly in smaller lots. And it is seamlessly linked with the tools now used by agile creators who can go from rough concept to polished prototype in the time it takes a big company to consider whether or not to make it. What's more, with cheap container shipping in an increasingly open global trade regime, anyone can send anything anywhere.

Factor in all these dimensions, and what does the future of manufacturing look like? Start-ups are not likely to start making airliners, but in anything less complex it is hard to argue that "big" is going to be a decisive advantage from here on. It is equally hard to argue that any single cost factor will continue to push all manufacturing activity to one corner of the globe, as labor has until now.

In light of these facts, it is hard not to conclude that the Earth is becoming flat . . . at least in manufacturing terms. What advantages are left? I see two as being critical: speed, both getting to market and in response to fluctuating demand, and impeccably elaborated creative genius.

It is not hard to see who is going to provide the creative genius and speed on the product development end: that requires the CAD skills that only 3 million people have so far. What is less clear is who is going to do the manufacturing, but I think we can point to some likely suspects:

- *Big companies* (at least some of them) may prove to be agile in adapting to a new world of open engineering and in adopting new approaches to manufacturing. In combination, dynamic research and development (R&D), massive global marketing power, and flexible manufacturing at sites close to customers around the world may give big players an enduring advantage. The big question is whether they can match smaller rivals in speed and creativity. What's going to be much more intriguing is to watch the progress of . . .

- *Small/medium-sized manufacturers* in the advanced economies may be up for a renaissance, if only because the new playing field addresses many of their long-term weaknesses. As the next generation of factory automation offers greater flexibility at lower cost, it is a chance to escape being stuck in a narrow niche serving a fixed client base—for example, being tied to Detroit's Big Three. Doing the same thing for decades leaves smaller shops with rigidly fixed ideas—"We make metal doors, not wood," as my first employer told me—and leaves them with stunted marketing capability. Happily, the Internet solves that by way of online marketplaces that put contract production opportunities in front of machine shops worldwide. Here again, CAD in the cloud is crucial because it gives prospective bidders a highly detailed spec to quote on and enables remote collaboration. In this way, we are going to see optimal matches between creators and producers.

So what we may see is product creators jobbing out fabrication work to one or more small contract manufacturers around the world. It may be a network of suppliers with production sites close to customers on each continent, or it may be a single source close to home. Wherever the work is done, clients are going to look much more closely over shoulders on the factory floor. To see why, witness the recent experience of major apparel brands with garments made in Bangladesh. In trying to audit labor standards compliance, many found they couldn't even tell where the work was actually happening.

Then again, if you want it done right. . . .

- *Do-it-yourself production* may be an increasingly attractive option for design-driven businesses, given increasingly affordable automated tooling seamlessly linked to CAD. In terms of continuous learning and control of quality, cost, inventory, and intellectual property, there may be no better way than to do it yourself. What's more, making it in-house and locally can add to the authenticity and cachet of your product. It may be the cool factor of California's surf culture or the traditional legacy of Vermont, the reputation for precision that goes with Swiss-made, or simply the hometown celebrity of the proprietor.

Not that you have to make all the components yourself. If manufacturing in the United States, you might get parts that are not expensive to keep in inventory—maybe the plastic case for your product—custom-fabricated in bulk in China or Mexico. Other more expensive components may be ordered off-the-shelf on a just-in-time basis to keep inventory costs down. What you want to do in-house is assembly—for the sake of quality control—and any processes that require your "secret sauce." The key is to keep inventory costs down while maintaining maximum flexibility to respond quickly to fluctuating demand.

Of course, the most persuasive reason why *not* to try making it yourself is that you don't know anything about manufacturing. But even that may be less of a barrier in future.

Making "The Old Man" Virtual

Manufacturing has always depended on what Nick Pinkston calls the old man—the veteran tool-and-die maker who shakes his head and tells the naïve young engineer that his design is difficult, if not impossible, to make. Across the United States, Japan, and Europe, we are losing these old guys as the massive wave of baby boomers hits retirement. So it has become an urgent software development imperative to digitize their skills before they disappear.

The anticipated result is artificial intelligence tools that will shift accumulated craft knowledge from the factory floor to the engineering design team. Even better, this digitized craft expertise will be directly linked to all those new flexible, automated, and intelligent tools coming down the pipe—and to CAD.

This is just one example of the kinds of artificial intelligence tools that will support decision making in future manufacturing. Benchmarking databases will help identify suboptimal error rates and material wastage. Sourcing engines will help product developers locate materials or the best possible prices for contract manufacturing. You can already consult online quoting engines, but the results are pretty crude and so far useful mainly as reference rates. In the future, ever more sophisticated decision-making tools are going to support the where-to-build decision. And the collective experience of the networked engineering community is going to spotlight both negative and positive outcomes.

What's the Outcome?

With so many factors of the manufacturing equation thrown into flux, the outcome is hard to predict . . . and I hate to make predictions.

Nick Pinkston believes that digital manufacturing will give rise to new verticals: production tightly integrated from the designer's CAD screen to the numerically controlled and networked flexible tooling on the factory floor—making manufacturing an extension of the engineering design process. I'd buy that.

Assuming the same fast progression to commoditization we have seen with every other form of digital hardware, this may put the means of production within wider reach. That is to say, we could arrive at the point where the capital cost of setting up an automated factory is within the grasp of any young engineer with an idea brilliant enough to attract a modest amount of venture or angel capital—or to get a bank loan. It is also clear that the factory of the future will have more machines and fewer people on the floor.

Combine the two, and what do you get? Maybe brilliant young Hmong- and Somali-American engineers in Minneapolis getting their entire extended families to work in small flexible shops.

What is clear, to me at least, is that the revolution in progress is going to open the doors to new players inspired by engineering brilliance and entrepreneurial energy. Yes, perhaps this revolution will bring manufacturing back to the United States, which is fine by me. Either way, I'm encouraged to imagine how it will empower young engineers in places where mechanical engineering and manufacturing have never fully flourished before: Uganda, Uruguay, Uzbekistan, and U-tell-me-where-else.

The bottom line on a flat planet is that the future winners in manufacturing are going to be people who passionately live and breathe to make things. You tell me: Do Americans still have that kind of passion?

Executive Takeaways

Manufacturing is a unique activity that involves issues that other businesses may not face. At the same time, the changes in manufacturing can offer lessons for other sectors.

- What are the "guilds" in your industry? Do you see groups that don't play well together?

- Do you see knowledge that one guild has that would make the other more effective? If so, what could you change to make it easier for that knowledge to flow more freely?

- If your organization uses outside suppliers for certain tasks, do you see hidden costs in those relationships? What could you do to highlight and minimize those costs?

- What are the economies of scale in your industry? Are any of them likely to diminish as the world gets more tightly connected and communication becomes easier?

- Who is the old man in your organization? How can you make that knowledge accessible to everyone in your company?

8 Marketing

Engineers Can Do It Better

At the start of the previous chapter I told you, "At the end of the day, it's all about manufacturing." Although there *is* a lot of truth to that, it must be admitted that at the end of the *quarter*, it's all about how many units you were able to actually sell in the past three months.

If we engineers sometimes lose sight of that bottom line, it's perhaps because—in our minds, at least—the people in marketing inhabit the same netherworld as human resources, compliance, and legal. You only want to meet them when it is absolutely unavoidable.

During the initial weeks in my first job at the aforementioned door manufacturer in Estonia, I used to wonder why there was always a line of people sitting for hours on a bench outside the engineering office, looking like they were waiting to see a dentist. When I finally asked why, I learned that they were all sales and marketing people who were patiently waiting their turn to see the engineers. "Why are we wasting their time?" I thought. "Surely there is a better way to do this."

That was my first experience with the bottleneck that I've since encountered in manufacturing enterprises around the world. Information that is critical to marketing and sales functions, and to customers, remains unnecessarily bottled up in engineering. And that is our bad.

What my sales colleagues in Estonia needed to know from the engineers was mostly whether their customers could get some small modification to the doors they wanted to order and how much it would cost. For the marketing people, it was often about the photorealistic renderings they needed to illustrate their product catalogs.

At the age of 24, I was put in charge of information technology (IT) and realized that design software had the power to break these choke points. With the sales reps, the fact that only the engineers had access to our product data was causing three problems. First, the "well-behaved" salespeople were wasting the engineers' time by asking questions such as, "Can we make a door modified to this customer's specification?" Second, the "bad boy" salespeople—who were actually the ones who brought in the most business—would just go ahead and sign deals for whatever the customer asked for. Inevitably, it was not until the day before deadline that we discovered they had committed us to a door height taller than the standard-size sheet metal plates that we used. The third problem was that our processes were not standardized, so everyone did whatever they liked and left it to the engineers and factory workers to figure it out. That is how I almost got punched out by the Ukrainian welder.

We solved all three problems by integrating the product data with the software tools that the sales team used. This ensured that they could sell only products that were actually possible to manufacture. Once we started using these templates, our manufacturing efficiency improved dramatically. The overall impact was huge: We freed up engineering time, we made the process much better, and our customers were happier because, suddenly, we started to keep our promises.

That got the sales team off the bench in our waiting room, but the marketing people were still there. Then one day it really hit me. I realized that we could solve a lot more problems by making the engineering data more accessible. So I began to pester the engineers, asking them over and over: "What task in your day most annoys you?" Of course, that gave them an opening to respond: "Talking to *you* is the most annoying part of my day."

Finally, though, one of the engineers admitted that he felt it was a waste of his time to create photorealistic renderings for the marketing department. "I'm an engineer, not an artist," he complained. So I began to look for a way that the marketing people could do it by themselves. Back then, though, solving the problem was tough because the rendering functionality was buried deep inside the computer-aided design (CAD) software. Nevertheless, the challenge fascinated me, and I became intrigued by the potential for CAD to make the entire process from design through manufacturing more collaborative and more efficient. In fact, it was that insight that set me on the path to where I am now.

As Close as Lips and Teeth

In the 10 years since then, a lot of change has occurred within our profession, mostly resulting from the huge leaps in the capability of our CAD tools. But technical progress has not been matched by an increase in collaboration between engineering and marketing. In an era of ever-shorter product cycles, that has to end. The two disciplines must be, as Mao Zedong used to say, "as close as lips and teeth." How can we make that happen?

Skullcandy, the wonderfully named Utah outfit that has made headphones into hot fashion items (see the following feature), puts its designers and marketers in the same room to quickly churn out an endless array of fresh designs. That has upped the ante from "gotta have that brand" to "gotta have *this week* from that brand." Plus it means that every kid in the same high school class can wear Skullcandy without looking like a clone.

Skullcandy: The Sound of Seamless Design and Marketing

If you want to know what the new breed of manufacturing start-up looks like—driven by twin engines of rapid product development and marketing—check out Skullcandy, the ultra-stylish maker of personal audio devices. It was founded in 2003; it has an edgy name that no Fortune 500 CEO would ever sign off on; it employs just over 200 people; it is based in Park City, Utah . . . which is not exactly the center of the universe; and it is a global leader in its category. This is what disruptive looks like.

Ten years on, Skullcandy is known for the ultra-cool, youthful sports and music design of its earphones (over-ear, on-ear, or earbud) and accessories. Out of the start-up gate, its core proposition was patented technology that allows the same device to work with both mobile phones and music players. Now Skullcandy is also big in gaming and sells to more than 80 countries around the world through specialty action sports and youth lifestyle retailers, big-box consumer electronics retailers (including Best Buy and Target), Apple stores, and of course its own website. Net sales in 2011 (the latest year available) reached $232.5 million—more than a million bucks per employee.

Skullcandy designs speak to sports, music, and fashion enthusiasts, amplified by endorsements from the stars of skateboarding, snowboarding, skiing, surfing, and various motorcycle racing formats, plus top professional basketball and American football players; musical acts, including Metallica, Jay Z, and Snoop Dogg; and, last but not least, supermodels, including Kate Upton, Chanel Iman, Chrissy Teigen, and Jessica Stam. Now that I think about it, their ratio of endorsing celebrities to actual employees is probably without parallel.

Its young customers are fanatically eager to make a fashion statement in having the coolest and latest gear—and for kids today that means this month not last month. On one hand they want what everyone else has; on the other hand, they don't want to look like fashion clones. If you want to stay on top of this demanding demographic, you have to move fast.

Dave Vogt, an industrial designer on the Skullcandy team, says: "Swift product innovation centered around our consumers is key to our success so far, and to the continued growth of our brand . . . which is all about style and innovation. Our customers are passionate enthusiasts, in pursuit of the latest in colors, styles, and audio quality, with a strong emotional connection to our products. So consumer feedback is a huge focus for us. Skullcandy consumers connect with our brand identity and our commitment to giving them what they want—great-looking, cool products that offer the latest in audio technology and user

(*continued*)

(*continued*)

experience. For us, every product begins and ends with the consumer in mind."

Each product also begins in three-dimensional (3D) CAD, which Dave cites as integral to Skullcandy's brand and processes, from design and prototyping though to marketing. It is the key to speed. "We are driven by youth culture and fashion. Our ability to develop and launch cool, fun, and exciting next-level products quickly—products that keep us top of mind with our consumers—is critical," says Dave. "So our marketing, graphic design, and industrial design teams work, literally, in tandem across the corridor from one another, collaborating throughout the product development process."

As Skullcandy's 3D CAD design teams work on incorporating the latest technologies into their designs, they continually receive direction on trends in colors and materials from their graphic design and marketing colleagues. "This ability to capture the never-ending flow of ideas so quickly and integrate the audio technologies with trends is what keeps our brand new and exciting," Dave says.

He adds, "Our drive to maintain a meaningful exposure to the upcoming trends, plus our focus on our consumers, and folding their tastes and preferences into our product development loop . . . this is what sets us apart from the competition. We have integrated the powerful capabilities of 3D CAD technology to facilitate and build on our integrated approach to delivering on our promise to our customers."

The ability to rapidly iterate fresh designs and prototypes allows Skullcandy to offer "a myriad of styles, colors,
and attitudes." Its customizable Aviator line, for example,
allows consumers to choose colors of the headphone's
headband, frame, caps, and cord. This trend to self-
expression, Dave speculates, may play a big part as technologies continue to evolve. "Who knows what the future
will bring . . . but we are dedicated to bringing what we're
known for—supreme sound and distinctive styling—to
the consumer audio market for years to come."

Even through the public relations–speak of an e-mail
interview, what comes through in communicating with
Skullcandy is the intensity of its focus. That's how a team
of just 200 people can set the pace in a global marketplace—and it may just be the template for a new breed
of manufacturer that leverages 3D CAD collaboration to
integrate strengths in design and engineering with powerful marketing—all at high speed.

The shared "room" you create for engineers, designers, and
marketers no longer needs to be physical, nor do you have to
make everyone move to Utah. Cloud-based engineering tools
now make it easy for stakeholders on all sides—and from distant
markets—to collaborate with full bandwidth in real time.

Rapid variation and customization is one good reason to
bring design and marketing closer together, and it's gotten much
easier to iterate rapidly through both design and manufacture.
On the design end, the small tweak that used to take half a day
to redraw can now be done in 15 minutes. In manufacturing,

flexible tooling in the plant can often interpret and execute the revised spec with minimal set-up time. As a result, in many companies the biggest remaining barrier is lack of collaboration.

Here again, the emerging trend favors businesses that manufacture close to their customers—in other words, not at the other end of a supply chain stretching all the way to China. It provides an excellent opportunity to exploit the inherent advantage of being able to deliver custom product quickly and at no extra cost. Yet I still see marketers penalizing customers who want customization with extra charges, when custom service should be their unique selling point (USP).

One of the best examples of what is now possible is in window shades and blinds. Even if you live in a funky old New England house with odd-sized windows, you can just take the measurements down to a franchise outlet such as Blinds To Go, where you can see and feel hundreds of styles and options—or you can shop online. When you place your order, it goes straight to the factory, where it is made to your spec and delivered within days by courier.

Sure, life is simpler for the manufacturer if everyone takes the same size and color. Yes, you can run into inventory and purchasing problems if your option menu gets too complex. Some components may impose physical limits. With patio doors, for example, scope for customization is limited by the available sizes of tempered glass plates. What's more, you can point to failed examples of mass customization, such as the build-to-order system that Dell pioneered in building personal computers. It was technically brilliant, but ultimately customers simply did not need it. So increased customization is not the answer in every business. It is, however, an example of the kind of cross-functional exploration that should be encouraged.

Make Your Engineers Dance

Marketers, it's time to get your shy wallflower engineers out on the dance floor. Which is to say, make them the stars of your social media presence. For example, say you make those wonderful new multifunction coffee machines like the one by Keurig. We have one in our office, and with a room full of mechanical engineers, I am always afraid that one of them won't be able to resist the temptation to take it apart just to see what is inside. (Maybe we should put signs up telling them not to.) So on its website or Facebook page, why doesn't Keurig have its engineers explain what goes on inside? What was their eureka moment, the breakthrough that made it possible? What are they most proud of?

Getting the engineers onto social media is win-win for both functions. Marketing gets really solid content; the engineers get to feel the wind in their face: a real sense of how customers feel about the product. This can be particularly useful with business-to-business products where the manufacturer is separated from end users by the distribution chain. In a lot of cases, the users are technically minded people with a real interest in the guts of the machines they work with—which means they may have valuable insights to share.

I can't imagine any mechanical engineer objecting to this—after all, the products we design are like our children, and we want to know how they get along in the world.

Still, the real gem waiting inside our CAD programs for marketing to exploit is our art: the computer-generated imagery (CGI) that flows from the geometry we create in the design process. CAD has transformed mechanical engineers into artists, something no one could have imagined a generation ago when all we did was work with abstract blueprints.

Today, we routinely generate picture-perfect still images and animations in the course of our work, images of each individual part along with really cool versions that include cutaways and exploded views showing how all the pieces fit together. But often no one outside product development sees any of it.

Given that the capability to create photorealistic renderings has been available for more than a decade, it is surprising how few companies use them, especially considering that marketers almost invariably win business when they use this amazing tool. The problem is, again, that the data are locked up in a CAD program marketers can't access.

A few years ago, when GrabCAD was still a small community, we used to feature job postings in order to match customers with engineers who had the right skill set. One of the first companies to take advantage of this was Wermo, a custom furniture manufacturer. Wermo was hoping to win more bids by attaching a photorealistic rendering with every proposal. Not having the resources in-house, Wermo turned to our community for help, and last I heard, it worked out very well.

Experiences like this convinced me that we needed to create an open platform with a very simple user interface so that marketers could create renderings themselves, without burdening the engineers or compromising the underlying design files.

What can you do with this art and the underlying data? Have a look at what automakers are doing with their CAD data these days.

Put a Car on the Moon? Piece of Cake, Mate

Car companies will seemingly go to any length to show their new models zipping through stunningly scenic terrain: tearing across the desert, sure-footedly climbing steep alpine tracks, or perched on the rim of the Grand Canyon. But these days, they no longer have to actually go as far as you might imagine.

"Companies like Mazda used to actually airfreight cars from Japan all the way down to us here in Australia until around 2008," says Glenn Gibson, chief executive officer (CEO) of Bluefish, a Melbourne-based creative imaging specialist. "It was worth it because Australia offers a wide range of visually fresh and distinctive natural scenery, from the Outback and the jungle to the Snowy Mountains to the rugged seascapes of our Great Ocean Road. We've got it all."

He continues, "But gradually, after 2005, the way we work began to change as 3D CAD became more and more sophisticated and rendering tools matured. So what happens these days is that the car flies down here virtually—from Japan, India, Europe, or wherever—in the form of a massive CAD file—usually between 10 and 20 gigabytes—that includes every minute detail of the design, inside and out. From that we create CGI animations or stills that are absolutely faithful to the real thing in every detail."

So the cars we see in advertising nowadays are, more and more likely, no longer actual physical entities. They are photo-realistic CAD renderings indistinguishable from the real thing. I love it: CAD is reality! How far we've come. Not so long ago the "perfect matte" was the Holy Grail of imaging. But how does Bluefish mesh the CGI image with the background environment? And what about the scenery? Is that real? Glenn shares:

Oh, yeah, the scenery is real—genuine Australia or New Zealand. We still do car shoots, just using a stand-in instead of the car that's still being developed. We either shoot custom

*locations to brief or use location scenes from our CGI library. On
location, we shoot both back-plates and matching 360-degree
images, 32-bit spherical domes that become our lighting maps for
the CGI scene. We'll sometime use a "mule"—which is what we
call the stand-in vehicle—as this allows us to work with tracking rigs to achieve ultra-realistic background motion blur on the
back-plates. Sometimes we'll also use a helicopter with a team on
the ground shooting HDRI [high-dynamic-range imaging] domes
while the air crew shoots the back-plates. The mules can also give
us fixed data points, anchors, to which we can align the CGI in
relation to the background.*

*We might drive along a coast road, through a modern
cityscape or down a recently built highway overpass capturing
every detail along the way. But here's the tricky part: Every step of
the way, each moment, the light is changing, shadows are passing
across the vehicle and the glass, the chrome, and the paintwork—
all of which are reflecting the environment surrounding the car.
If we don't capture that data for real on location then you can't
match it in CGI. If we don't get that just right, you'll be able to
spot that it's not real, instantly.*

*This is where art takes over from science. We like to say that
our strength is that we are creatives who deeply understand
technology, not technicians trying to be creative. We were already
on top of our game as photographers when CGI came out, and it
takes years of experience to get that kind of understanding of light
and shadow. But we were also pretty tech-savvy by that time, so
we dug right in to CGI and learned how to use, control and
manipulate the CGI tools to our advantage.*

*We strive for reality in our work and go to great lengths to
achieve it with matched lighting domes shot at the same time as
backgrounds, but there's also a fine art to manipulating that to
make the product better. There's been many a time shooting real
cars on location over the years that once I have the car and background angle looking sensational, I've jokingly asked the assistant*

to rotate the Earth for me so the sun is 30 degrees left or right. That always got a laugh and onward we'd go, but I knew the car would look a zillion times better if we could actually rotate the planet. Well, in CGI world I can do just that.

You can judge for yourself how close Glenn and his team get toward a seamless match between CGI and background by looking at the portfolio on his website. But the seamless matte is not the only advantage Glenn sees in this magical extension of CAD:

The beauty of CGI is that your viewpoint can be absolutely anywhere; it's not restricted by the real-world physics that make positioning a camera 20 meters overhead a somewhat tricky proposition. Being able to look straight down in that way, along with the ability to merge exterior and interior data, allows us to create stunning cutaway views without destroying vehicles.

Better yet, we can use the interior data to make a fully navigable animation of the passenger compartment so you can poke around online looking at all the details of the dash and the seats . . . and really get a feel for the colors and textures. We can even use color configurators or other animation techniques so that people can play around with different styling options. This is a killer app for a marketing website . . . it turns brochure-ware into a very engaging experience with the product.

So is there anything Glenn can't do yet? Can he put an SUV on the moon?

"Piece of cake, mate," he assures me.

[As] long as you can get me the background imagery. Although, having said that, we are now increasingly creating backgrounds in CGI, especially when something more conceptual or stylistic is required, and where reality is not the ultimate objective. We

could probably do something credible with what NASA's got from the lunar rovers sent up so far. But next time they go to the moon I hope NASA will take along a hi-def, 360-degree spherical dome camera—and to Mars, too.

The Marketing Treasure in CAD

Having specialists such as Bluefish in the CAD space adds an amazing new dimension to open engineering, one that literally opens up a universe of possibility for marketing: Put your product on Mars if you like. But what I really like about Glenn's business is how he has been able to succeed in global markets from a base in Australia. He modestly says that his clients come for the Outback scenery, but by now the clients must be coming back because the team is bloody good, as the Aussies might put it. That is closely in sync with the phenomenon we are seeing at GrabCAD: CAD specialists everywhere from South Carolina to Serbia to Singapore are thriving on work from around the world. For me, this is the fulfillment of the dream that led me to start GrabCAD in the first place. I just wanted a way to get work from way over the horizon.

At the end of the day, the end of the quarter, and the end of the financial year, here are two things to remember about marketing and the revolution that 3D CAD is driving: (1) greater collaboration among design, manufacturing, and marketing is critically important, and (2) CAD can yield an incredible treasure to marketing by means of providing photorealistic rendering. And that treasure is there to be harvested from the earliest stages when a start-up is no more than a concept. As we have seen in earlier chapters, highly detailed and realistic CAD renderings can provide the magic ingredient in crowdfunding, consumer research, and prototyping. So, yes, this revolution is not just about engineering and design or prototyping and manufacturing. At the end of the day it's just as much about marketing.

Executive Takeaways

For manufacturers, it may be engineers and marketers who don't communicate. But every organization includes multiple cultures that don't always communicate effectively, and every company has customers who want something just a little bit different from everyone else.

- Who is the resource in your company that everyone lines up to see?

- What would happen if you put two groups that don't get along that well in the same room, as Skullcandy did?

- What part of your product or service would customers most like to customize? How could you achieve that?

9 The Puzzle Pattern Emerges

What you have read in the preceding chapters represents to me the many pieces of a large jigsaw puzzle, one with a pattern that is only now emerging. Three years ago I could see only two or three of the pieces and how they fit together: how the rise of cloud computing was going to amplify the growing power of computer-aided design (CAD) by ushering in a new software paradigm that will make wide-scale collaboration easier.

In the course of pursuing that vision over the 40 months or so since, I have come across a new piece of the puzzle almost every other month—and observed the momentum that is quickly aligning them to create (what is to me at least) the antithesis of the perfect storm. The wonder of that is what motivated me to write this book.

Forgive me if I have blown my own company's horn too often along the way, but it was hard to tell this story without describing why I was in a position to witness it. I hope that my account presents a clear, logical, and persuasive picture of the forces converging to reorder the way we design and make physical objects.

If all this seems obvious, it has not been until very recently. Even from the Olympian heights of GE's boardroom, the full scope and significance of what is just over the horizon was only becoming apparent in the fall of 2013.

We are on the verge of a revolution that is going to quickly and radically transform the way physical goods are designed, manufactured, and marketed—and how their development is funded. This revolution will reorder all our notions about making things: who designs and who builds it and how fast, where, and at what scale.

Is this a "good" thing? As with any radical transformation of this magnitude, there will be losers and unforeseen consequences. But if you are among those who hate to see the advantages of big get bigger, if you favor level playing fields and increased competition, if you think consumers deserve greater choice and power over producers, if the widespread flowering of individual creativity sounds positive to you . . . then, yes, this is a very, very good thing.

As a start-up entrepreneur from a tiny country that has only rejoined the world within my lifetime, I can say wholeheartedly, bring it on! This gives everyone, everywhere a fair chance to compete in the global economy.

Piece by Piece

Consider the pieces of the puzzle we can see at this point, how they are likely to fit together, and to whose advantage.

In the Factory

New production technologies such as additive manufacturing (three-dimensional [3D] printing, for example) and easy-to-train robots are making factories faster and more flexible. These new technologies are all numerically controlled, which means they can be instructed and monitored directly from a CAD screen, a screen that may be on the other side of the world. At the same time, the factory may no longer need to be on the other side of the world. With automation becoming both more productive and affordable and labor becoming more costly (even in China), the equation of location advantage becomes more complex—especially once you factor in the phenomenal logistical efficiency of modern container ships.

New Materials

A piece of the puzzle we have not even explored in this book is new materials. From ultra-high-strength/high-tensile steels to advanced carbon-fiber composites to bioengineered miracles such as yeasts that can be used to culture human tissue, materials science is rapidly extending the potential for innovation. Combine this with new CAD tools that allow engineers to rapidly simulate how these new materials will perform in real-world conditions and the door opens to quantum leaps. The way our GrabCAD community was able to slash the weight of GE's jet engine brackets shows just what is possible.

Prototyping and Testing

One freelance engineer with a credit card and a broadband connection to the cloud can now run advanced simulations that would have taken NASA a year and an army of engineers just one generation ago. This means designs can be rapidly elaborated to near-perfection in a virtual environment. "Getting physical" is now similarly easy. Start-ups can now do a lot on very little using do-it-yourself tools such as 3D printers to make molds or direct prototypes. Specialist prototyping shops offer more sophisticated tools and advice. All this means that product developers can now create hundreds of iterations on the road to producing a final polished prototype.

Funding and Marketing

Ralph Waldo Emerson was wrong: "Build a better mousetrap and the world will beat a path to your door"—*not*. Inventors and aspiring novelists used to have a lot in common: the rejection letters sent out by publishers and the turndowns from manufacturers afflicted by the "not invented here syndrome." Online innovation hubs such as Kickstarter and Quirky have changed that, decisively and forever—at least for inventors. Now there are diverse routes forward for those who have only a brilliant idea and for those who have the idea plus the skills to elaborate it. You can crowdfund development capital and crowdsource market research (and consumer demand) using amazingly realistic CAD renderings and animations. A monumental barrier to innovation has crumbled like the Berlin Wall.

Collaborative Power

The power of the crowd is just as much a factor in how the revolution is mobilizing engineers and designers. In our online community, we have directly experienced the power that flows when 700 engineers from around the world crowdswarm a single problem. GE has seen it, too. The massed power of diverse perspectives is one side of the coin. The other side is a potent new ability to source exactly the right engineer for the task at hand.

On another level is the newfound ease with which all stakeholders in a design process can actively contribute just-in-time value. A lone genius can do wonders in CAD today, but genius in teams is exponentially more powerful. Design teams are even more powerful if seamlessly linked with customers, managers, marketers, and makers. All of this is now possible like never before.

The Digital Force That Drives It Forward . . .

As I told you up front, this revolution is digital, the second wave of the revolution that transformed to digits every physical thing that could be. Behind every puzzle piece cited earlier, you can find the transformative force of information technology: the digitization of the factory, the near-infinite compute power that carries materials science forward, CAD software converging with cloud hardware to empower simulation and collaboration, and the new forms of social and economic organization enabled by the Internet.

On top of all that, get ready for the "Internet of Things." Chips and sensors are now so cheap that you can almost sprinkle them on your french fries (not to say they'd taste good). That gives this revolution its mission: to reinvent every possible device with connected intelligence that makes it greener, safer, more convenient and secure, remotely controllable . . . and harder to lose under a sofa cushion. We just have to figure out how to make it all hackproof.

The digital and information technology (IT) aspects of all this are not in doubt. We can see them coming or anticipate that massive progress lies ahead. For example, although it is not here yet, we can expect a massive surge in battery capability given the intense research and development efforts in that field. And we can be pretty certain that all these IT advances will be universally available. Everyone around the world will be competing with the same toolkit to choose from.

Go back and look at all the puzzle pieces laid out throughout this book . Consider carefully their significance and how they fit together, because that is the second-most important point of this book. Do you see how any combination of these pieces delivers a decisive advantage to anyone? Because I don't. The playing field looks level and democratized to me.

So what will separate the winners from the losers in this revolution? (If this were television we would break for a commercial right now.)

. . . And the Decisive Factor That Will Determine the Winners

Here is the most vital thing to remember from this book: CAD now concentrates previously inconceivable creative power on an individual computer screen. Anyone can buy all the kit needed to leverage this power from home for less than the price of a new compact car.

It is the power to give virtual form and functionality to anything you can imagine; to validate it with incredible sophistication, virtually and physically; and to visualize it with the power to attract capital and sales. It is capability that can reach as far as a factory floor on the other side of the world.

For this reason, the pivotal joint at the very center of this revolutionary jigsaw puzzle is where the power of CAD interlocks with the creative capacity of the human talent that drives it.

But here is the bad news. If you have no inspiration, CAD will not transform you into a genius. If you have no grasp of mathematics or engineering principles or if you have no aptitude or skill for designing and making things, then this is not for you. If you have not done your homework, CAD will not do it for you. Don't lose heart entirely, though: You still may be able to hire people who paid attention in class.

This is where we get to the truly decisive question: Who and where will the talent be?

Unlike the march of digital technology progress, the future outlook on the CAD talent front is not at all clear. And few vantage points offer a clear perspective. Even the CAD software makers—isolated from their customers by networks of so-called value-added resellers (VARs)—can't see very deep into the talent pool. I had to do a lot of digging just to get the estimate that there are just 3.1 million licensed 3D CAD users worldwide. The geographic distribution of CAD users is even tougher to fathom. The best estimates we have seen say the global population divides roughly one-third each in the Americas, Europe/Africa, and Asia-Pacific.

This is another reason I felt compelled to come forward and write this book. Observing the exponential growth of our now million-strong GrabCAD community has given me a unique bird's-eye perspective on who today's talent is and where they live. Since our interface is still entirely in English there is, of course, an inherent language bias, which is why we still have relatively few members in China and Japan. The top five nations where our members live are the United States, India, the United Kingdom, Brazil, and Germany.

When it comes to talent, quality of course trumps quantity. But if you read closely through the profiles of our engineers in Chapter 3 you will remember that we have many brilliant engineers in places such as Brazil, India, Greece, and Serbia. No matter where they live, these talented individuals are a global resource. Many are eager to work for clients on the other side of the planet.

As the revolution gathers momentum, though, we are going to need more and more CAD talent with all the proficiency we can give them. Where will we find them?

A disturbing insight discussed in Chapter 3 comes from the observations of one young engineer after another about the quality of CAD training today. I have yet to hear anyone rave about the courses available from the VARs. Many likewise complain that their engineering school instructors don't even know how to use CAD, much less train anyone else. That's why upcoming stars such as Chris Shakal and William Barclay end up teaching their fellow students what they have learned from our community.

This deficiency points to an urgent mission for companies, communities, and countries. The coming generation of CAD-equipped engineers and designers will drive this revolution. Some will, no doubt, work remotely for companies on the other side of the world. Many more will ensure the growth and per-haps survival of existing companies closer to home. Others will be among the founders of start-ups that build prosperity in their hometowns.

So the winners in this revolution are likely to be the indi-viduals, the companies, the communities, and the countries with the best and most CAD talent in the future. And it won't just grow; it must be cultivated.

Where is that talent right now? It is in elementary or middle school among kids who are maybe 10 to 15 years old and already heavily involved with computers.

How can we channel their enthusiasm into CAD? Here is where to start. . . .

End the Senseless Zombie Slaughter

If today's teenagers around the world were McDonald's, their collective boast would not be "Burgers: billions and billions served," it would be "Zombies: billions and billions slaughtered"—plus monsters, terrorists, and sundry other bad guys. To what end? Too many video games today are just senseless mayhem.

This is not a trivial tangent, because if you go back to Chapter 3 and read what led our current crop of young stars into CAD, you will find a consistent answer: They started at a young age playing with LEGO, the plastic building blocks that are Denmark's greatest contribution to global civilization.

Building objects as play seems to trigger a specific kind of imagination and creativity that some people are born with. A generation ago, many of those who had it would graduate from LEGO to building model airplanes and such. This was a great activity in terms of developing small motor skills and patience—and it inspired many people to become engineers. In another sense it was kind of passive in that teens didn't learn much about the science behind the designs (unless they were motivated to read books about it).

Today, young kids (and their parents) still play with LEGO and other building toys, but at a certain age, most children now seem to drift into zombie slaughter, which is a shame and a waste. Instead, video games could and should be offering young minds so much more: a direct route to learning productive and valuable CAD skills. If truth be told, 3D CAD is actually nothing more than the world's most amazing video game.

The intriguing potential of CAD as play is that you can start off doing things that are fairly easy but still fun and rewarding.

As you progress, you hit walls that require your skills to grow. I imagine 14-year-olds, firmly hooked on CAD play, reaching the point where they say, "Omigawd, I need to know about geometry to go further!"—or physics, or perspective drawing . . . CAD has the potential to stimulate desire to master all of those subjects that many teens find boring. (Personally, I loved both math and physics.)

So far, the only game I have found that does anything like this is Minecraft, from Swedish game developer Markus Persson. (Everything good comes from Northern Europe.) But there is room for much, much more development in this field.

The real challenge is to find a way to engage girls in CAD. And as the father of two young daughters, I hope someone comes up with an answer in the next five years. From what we can see in our community, something like 90 percent of CAD practitioners are male, and that's an immense problem. Trying to design products without a female perspective is like operating with only half a brain. And where the goal is to design products to meet specifically female needs and tastes, it is a no-brainer.

Game developers may well play a major role in the progress of this revolution, but ultimately it is up to parents and educators to produce the talent that will direct its course.

The Winning Hand?

On an individual level, of course, you can't force anyone to learn, especially those with no aptitude, inspiration, or passion. Likewise, it is difficult to predict that society will win unless it attaches value to both education and making things. Still, it will take more than that to win in this revolution.

Countries such as Finland (and Estonia), which excel in high school math and science, have some good cards in their hand. Nations such as Japan, with its legendary diligence and reverence for *monozukuri bunka*, the "culture of making things," will no doubt be strong contenders. India, despite its creaking systems, will likely continue to produce more than its share of brilliant engineers.

What about the United States? Whatever its weaknesses in high-school math or the preference of its young for jobs on Wall Street, as I have discovered, America has one amazingly powerful asset: phenomenal entrepreneurial energy and a bias for innovation over tradition. In many other lands that is sadly lacking.

What other country has that kind of entrepreneurial energy, plus high math scores? China, which—even on a more level playing field—is going to be a formidable competitor whatever happens.

This is not to say that this is going to be a case of winner-take-all. In the nineteenth century it used to be that manufacturing flourished where coal, iron ore, and limestone could converge to make steel, and from it ships and locomotives. In this century, we can expect manufacturing to flourish where design talent and entrepreneurial energy converge. And that can be anywhere . . . maybe even once again in Glasgow, the cradle of modern mechanical engineering.

On the corporate level, winners and losers are even tougher to predict.

Until now, "big" has had a decisive advantage given the immense financial resources and thousands of engineers needed to develop many kinds of new products and the thousands more factory workers needed to produce them. Over the course of a century, organizational models have developed with slight differences from the United States to Germany to Japan, but everywhere the process of big has required regimentation and long, time-consuming chains of command.

A vastly different approach to making things is now emerging, one that shifts the emphasis to flexibility and speed, one that requires fewer people, one in which the sinews between various functions need no longer be physical or permanent. In response, a new model or models of social organization will be needed.

With organizations specifically designed to prevent change, will big companies be able to adapt far enough and fast enough? Some will, no doubt. And those that produce complex, capital-intensive goods such as jet aircraft may be safely above the floodwaters. But absent some compelling rationale for their size, I think we can safely predict that many of today's giants are headed for extinction.

Nimble new developers and makers are already beginning to mushroom, because they can. A small team of engineers with minimal funding can design a sophisticated product within weeks. Or an entrepreneur with cash and the same idea can find a team online to do it. No more pleading with the banks; you can now crowdsource the funds to build it yourself or have it built in China. With a minimal budget and some inspired guerilla marketing, you can create a viral sensation on the Internet.

The barriers are eroding fast just as creators begin to realize they have at hand tools with unprecedented power. The puzzle is almost complete and revolution is coming.

APPENDIX
MEET THE CADOPOLY

If you want to buy a 3D CAD or PLM system, you have to choose one of four giant vendors: Dassault Systèmes, Autodesk, PTC, or Siemens PLM.

Dassault Systèmes SA

The maker of CATIA 3D CAD started as a business unit of the French aerospace group that makes the Mirage fighter aircraft. Today it offers two 3D CAD platforms: CATIA and SolidWorks, the latter developed by the eponymous Massachusetts-based company Dassault acquired in 1997. The two platforms are not compatible. Dassault is second to Siemens PLM in enterprise-class CAD/PLM systems, with a corporate client base that includes Boeing, Airbus, Bombardier, Ford, Toyota, Honda, Renault, and some divisions at Lockheed Martin. SolidWorks is the best-selling mainstream 3D CAD product, besting rival products from Autodesk, Siemens PLM, and smaller vendors.

Established: 1981, business unit of Dassault Group

HQ: Vélizy-Villacoublay, France (southwest of Paris) and Waltham, Massachusetts (SolidWorks)

Leader: Bernard Charlès, president and chief executive officer (CEO); Bertrand Sicot, CEO SolidWorks

Employees: 10,122 (as of 2012)

Key product lines: CATIA (CAD), SolidWorks (CAD), SIMULIA (physical simulation and analysis), DELMIA (factory simulation), ENOVIA (data management)

Annual revenue: 2.28 billion Euros (as of 2012)

Companies: SIMPOE, SFE, Netvibes, Exalead, Intercim, SolidWorks

Acquired: Gemcom, Safe Technology, Enginuity, many others

Strengths: With the exception of SolidWorks and some recent acquisitions, all products from the various divisions of Dassault Systèmes work very closely together. Customers usually choose Dassault Systèmes as an all-encompassing technology partner more than simply selecting from its portfolio of products, and they expect a high level of support.

Autodesk Inc.

Based in San Francisco and nearby San Rafael, California, Autodesk is the most diversified vendor in the CAD industry. It is traditionally strong in architecture and civil engineering because of the overwhelming acceptance of AutoCAD in the late 1980s and early 1990s, and it's still a best seller today.

Established: 1982

HQ: San Rafael, California

Leader: Carl Bass, president and CEO

Employees: 7,500

Key products: AutoCAD/AutoCAD LT, Revit, Inventor, Maya, 3ds Max, SketchBook, Alias Studio

Annual revenue: $2.3 billion (as of fiscal 2013)

Companies: Generic Software, Softdesk, Alias, Revit, Softimage

Acquired: Genius CAD, Ithaca Software, CAiCE, Buzzsaw, Navisworks, Skymatter, Algor, Moldflow, many others

Strengths: Architecture, civil engineering, plant design, mechanical design, and media 3D content creation; despite the growth of 3D for design, more than half the company's revenue still comes from AutoCAD.

PTC (Formerly Parametric Technology Corporation)

Boston-based PTC has been a leader in 3D CAD since it burst on the scene with its 1987 launch of Pro/Engineer, the first 3D CAD program to use parametric, feature-based associative modeling. In 2010 PTC renamed its expanded CAD product line (which by then included CoCreate, a 3D direct modeling product) to Creo. It also publishes Windchill, the third leading enterprise-class PLM system. PTC has major clients in all branches of heavy industry, as well as in consumer product goods, high-tech, and medical products.

Established: 1985

HQ: Needham, Massachusetts

Leader: James E. Heppelmann, CEO

Employees: 5,900 (as of 2013)

Key products: Creo, Windchill, Arbortext, Servigistics, Mathcad, and others

Annual revenue: $1.25 billion (as of 2012)

Companies acquired: CoCreate, Arbortext, Servigistics, Computervision, Mathsoft, ITEDO, Relex Software

Strengths: A large loyal customer base; willingness to enter new markets; Windchill PLM won a highly publicized new account in EADS, the parent company of Airbus, following a lengthy evaluation cycle in which it was compared to Dassault Systèmes ENOVIA and Siemens PLM Teamcenter.

Siemens PLM Software

Today's Siemens PLM Software started in 1963 as United Computing. Through decades of mergers, acquisitions, and changes in ownership it has become a strategic business unit within Siemens Industry Automation. Although Siemens is a public company, the PLM division is such a small part of its total business that very little financial information specific to the PLM division is released. The two flagship products are NX, a new-generation 3D CAD system based on the company's Parasolid 3D kernel, and Teamcenter, a PLM system with more than 7 million licensed seats—more than all PLM competitors combined. Key customers include General Motors, Chrysler, Daimler AG, NASA, BAE Systems, Fokker, and some divisions at Lockheed Martin. Co-ownership of the historic NASTRAN code for product analysis and simulation also makes it a major player in simulation.

Established: 1963

HQ: Plano, Texas

Leader: Chuck Grindstaff, CEO

Employees: 6,800 (2013 estimate)

Key products: NX (3D CAD), Solid Edge (mainstream 3D CAD), Teamcenter (PLM), Tecnomatix (factory simulation), NX Nastran and Femap (simulation), Parasolid (3D kernel)

Annual revenue: $3 billion (estimated 2012 earnings)

Companies acquired: Unigraphics, Applicon, SDRC, Vistagy, Tecnomatix, LMS, VRcontext

Strengths: Market leader Teamcenter is the PLM standard even for manufacturers who use CATIA or Creo CAD; parent company Siemens is a major customer, yet many divisions have not yet standardized on products from the PLM division, giving it a growth opportunity its competitors lack.

ACKNOWLEDGMENTS

This book wouldn't have seen the light of day without my wife, Laura, and daughters, Lana and Mona. They put up with me spending evenings and weekends working on this book (and on GrabCAD) instead of spending time with them.

I want to thank the fantastic GrabCAD community and customers; they are a constant source of inspiration for me.

Special thanks to my friend John Harris, a Canadian journalist and speechwriter, who helped turned my Estonian English into perfect English.

Thanks to Rob Stevens for managing the book project. Without him this book would not be in your hands, and John and I would be still brainstorming in his treehouse in Japan. Thanks also to the rest of book team—Madonna McManus, David M. Scott, Andy Payne, and Mike Volpe.

This book was only possible because of the many people who gave generously of their time, including the following: Carl Bass, Terry Stonehocker, Andreas Gkertsos, Chris Shakal, Venkatasubramanian, William Barclay, Sasank Gopinathan, Tommy Mueller, Verislav Mudrak, Nediane Mesquita, Jenny Tseitlin, Krista Casal, Paolo Termini, Alex Tepper, Nicholas Oxley, Nate Siress, Tony Slavik, Dulcie Madden, Nick Pinkston, Scott Miller, Herman Pang, Glenn Gibson, and Dave Vogt.

I also want to say thank you to my engineering professors Rein Küttner and Martin Eerme, who introduced me to CAD—in some sense, that's where this story started. Also to Mati Toomla and Riho Vask, who were my mentors at my first job as an engineer.

Thanks to all the people who first believed in me and shared my vision of how engineering was changing—Andrus Oks, Marek Kiisa, Katie Rae, Reed Sturtevant, Lee Hower, Axel Bichara, Izhar Armony, and Doron Rueveni. And especially to David Skok who was not only one of our first investors but who has been a great mentor to me over the years.

And finally thank you to the whole GrabCAD team who come to work every day trying to make engineers' lives better.

INDEX